Errata

Preface

p. v, line 7: "There, in an Indiana criminal court (see Figure 1), the" should read "There, in an Indiana criminal court, the"

Chapter 1

p. 10, line 7: "Koo's Kennedy Avenue office (see Figure 2)." should read "Koo's Kennedy Avenue office (see Figure 1)."

Chapter 2

p. 24, line 20: "Number 1 (see Figure 2)." should read "Number 1 (see Figure 1)."

Licensed

to

Rape?

John A. Sullivan

Learning Publications, Inc.
Holmes Beach, Florida

ISBN 1-55691-145-9

Learning Publications, Inc.
5351 Gulf Drive
P.O. Box 1338
Holmes Beach, FL 34218-1338

Printing: 5 4 3 2 1   Year: 3 2 1 0 9

Printed in the United States of America

Contents

Preface

On July 13, 1992, in the Superior Court of Lake County, in Crown Point, Indiana, a jury was impaneled to hear case number 45G-01-9101-CF-00006 — the State *v.* Young Soo Koo, a Korean medical doctor charged with the felony rape of a 28-year-old female patient during a pelvic examination at the doctor's office in Hammond, Indiana.

There, in a rural Indiana criminal court (see Figure 1), the author and his fellow jurors watched and listened as a pandora's box was opened before them, its vile contents spewing in every direction.

Day after day, witness after witness, the members of that jury were inexorably drawn into the emotional maelstrom of a well-meaning society gone terribly out of control.

This book examines abuses of a doctor-patient relationship that included statutory rape, felony rape, sexual molestation, narcotics to induce patient dependency, use of insurance and welfare funds to buy drugs for resale, and a host of fraudulent billing practices tolerated by the medical profession, government officials, insurance companies, and the voting public.

While intended primarily for rape victims, rape crisis workers, therapists, and legal case workers, Licensed to Rape? offers all readers a disturbing view of contemporary society.

Readers will also be made aware of the many roadblocks that were placed in the path of a young, unemployed mother who had the strength, courage, and determination to come forward to testify against such a respected "pillar of the community" as a doctor.

To supplement his personal experience as a member of the jury, the author interviewed the trial judge, the lead detective, the prosecutor, selected jurors, and the plaintiff. He attended three post-trial events and copied key trial transcripts.

The plaintiff's name is used with permission. The names of some of the victims have changed in order to protect the privacy of the individuals.

Introduction

Our jury of eight men and four women, plus a male alternate and a female alternate, was selected in a long session held on Monday, July 13, 1992 — three years, three months, and 14 days after Tammy Spasske's last visit to Dr. Young Soo Koo. She was experiencing her usual series of symptoms — cramping, bloating, and a vaginal discharge. Ever since the birth of her daughter she had been in and out of Dr. Koo's office more times than she could remember. He was her family physician and had treated her for over 10 years. Until recently she had complete confidence in him — both as a doctor and as a friend of the family.

But two weeks earlier he had done something during a pelvic examination that he had never done with her before. She had felt his fingers moving around the lips of her vagina in a seemingly non-medical manner. She assumed it to be some new medical procedure, but it still bothered her.

Thus it was with apprehension that she undressed from the waist down, wrapped a paper modesty drape about herself, and sat on the edge of the examination table to wait for the doctor.

When Dr. Koo entered the room he took her right arm in his hand and administered an injection. When she questioned him he said, "Don't worry; make you feel good, make you relax."

Never before had she received an injection just prior to a pelvic exam. Still, this was her family doctor and she could think of no reason not to trust him. So she ignored this warning signal, much as she had ignored the one two weeks earlier.

Because of that, and her failure to remove herself at once from the doctor's office, a jury was selected to determine what really happened in the next five minutes.

It is the nature of our criminal justice system that jurors hear a case five times. While it may seem excessively repetitive, it does tend to fix in the minds of each juror those elements of the case essential to a just verdict.

In his opening statement the prosecutor will tell the jury what he intends to prove and how he intends to prove it — element by element. The defense attorney then tells the jury that the State's evidence is either incorrect or insufficient to establish the guilt of his client beyond a reasonable doubt. He will cover the same elements addressed by the prosecution. Thus the case is presented to the jury from two points of view.

The testimony of all witnesses and the presentation of all exhibits by both sides constitute a third, and a complete, hearing of the case.

Final arguments simply go over the same ground as did the opening statements and testimony, highlighting those items of evidence that support one side or the other, and offer the jury a summary of the case from the two points of view. The jury is then ready to begin deliberations in search of a verdict.

1
In the Beginning

When jury selection was completed the judge introduced the principal players then present in the courtroom: Dr. Young Soo Koo, the defendant; John Breclaw, defense attorney; Jay Binder, an attorney assisting Mr. Breclaw; Philip Benson, a Lake County Deputy Prosecutor; Charles Hedinger, a detective sergeant with the Hammond, Indiana, Police Department assisting Mr. Benson; and, of course, himself — T. Edward Page.

Judge Page then informed the jury that the State of Indiana defined felony rape as "a penetration of the vagina by the penis under any one of three conditions: by force and against the will of the victim; when the victim is mentally deficient and does not understand what is happening; or when the victim is unaware of what is happening for any reason." He emphasized that Indiana law did not require ejaculation — penetration alone constituted rape if one of the above conditions was met.

He noted that the burden of proof rested solely with the prosecution; the defendant was not required to testify; jurors in criminal cases are not bound by the law — they have the legal right to reject it and construe it for themselves. He cautioned the jurors not to discuss the case with anyone — family members and fellow jurors included — until beginning deliberations.

July 14 • Tuesday • 10:15 a.m.

STATE ATTORNEY BENSON'S OPENING STATEMENT

May it please the court, counsel, ladies and gentlemen of the jury. We're here today because that man, Young S. Koo, is charged with rape — the rape of one of his patients of 10 years during an alleged pelvic examination.

You heard during the voir dire process about the elements of rape and how they apply in this case when the person raped was unaware that it was occurring.

The testimony from Tammy Spasske will be that that man was her doctor and her family's doctor for over 10 years, and that he treated her on a continual basis during that time span. She never had any problems, none whatever, with the treatment she received.

The rape occurred on March 30, 1989. Prior to that, Tammy Spasske had been having pelvic problems and numerous female problems. She had had D & Cs, laparoscopies — no ifs, ands, or buts. And this man, a general practitioner, continued to treat her for those severe pelvic problems. This continued on and on.

Ladies and gentlemen, in March of 1989, she had occasion to go to the defendant as she had been doing for years on a regular basis — sometimes as many as five, six times a month. She went to him on March 14 for problems in her stomach. His small office on Kennedy Avenue has two examination rooms, a doctor's office in the back, a waiting area, and a reception area.

On the fourteenth she saw the defendant and he told her to remove her clothes from the waist down as he needed to do an exam. When he left the room she undressed and got on the table. This exam table, she'll tell you, is flat with stirrups at the end to hold a female patient's feet so as to allow an examination of the genital area.

She'll testify that there is a light that overhangs the table, and that the doctor would hand her a paper sheet to drape over herself — to wrap around her waist.

This time, as in the past, the doctor came back after she was on the table with her feet in the stirrups and flat on her back and he took the corner of that sheet and taped it to the light overhanging the table. This would completely obstruct her view. She could not see him at all, no part of him.

She'll testify that when the doctor began the pelvic exam he put something inside her that was very cold and very hard, and he opened it up and it hurt. It hurt like all past pelvic exams; and she had had numerous pelvic exams. She will also testify to having sex on previous occasions before this pelvic exam.

What she felt is commonly called a speculum, a device that doctors use to open up the female vagina to look inside. This time she felt the defendant moving his fingers along the lips of her vagina — before, during, and after this exam — and it felt unlike anything she had ever felt from any doctor, including the defendant.

She thought this was strange, but this had been her doctor for 10 years. She'll tell you she went home and mentioned it to her mom that this was a little strange. She felt the doctor did something he shouldn't, but her mother reassured her that it was probably just her imagination.

She mentioned him being the family doctor for 10 years and that he would never do anything to hurt her.

To a certain extent Tammy dismissed the incident. She wanted to believe that her doctor would never do something like this. That was on March 14.

On March 28, she went back to the doctor. He had said to come back in two weeks if she didn't feel better. Now she had bloating in her stomach and pains that didn't go away.

Once again, in the examination room, there was no third party or nurse present. She unzipped her pants and lifted her shirt for the doctor to press in various ways on her stomach. He said that x-rays were needed and wrote a prescription for them.

Since she had problems with her breast she asked the doctor for a prescription for a mammogram at the same time. After a brief discussion the doctor included a prescription for the mammogram.

She had the x-rays taken at Munster Hospital at 1:30 p.m. on March 29, 1989. Later she called the doctor about the results and was told to come into his office before 3:00 p.m. on March 30.

She'll tell you she wasn't feeling well that day as the pain was continual. She signed in with the receptionist and the doctor took her into examination room number two, the room farthest from the reception area and behind examination room number one.

The doctor told her to prepare for another pelvic exam, the second in one month. She undressed from the waist down — the doctor having left the room as he always did — and she took the sheet and wrapped it around her lap and got up on the table in a sitting position.

The doctor came back in, and without any warning, not so much as even a "hello," grabbed her right arm and injected her. She'll tell you she never had any injection in her arm ever before from the doctor; injections were always in the hip and buttocks region. And she asked the doctor, "What was that?"

He says, "Don't worry, make you relax, make you feel good."

He had her lay on the exam table, put her feet in the stirrups, slide to the end of the table and position herself for a pelvic exam.

Then he took the sheet that was wrapped around her waist and taped it to the light that directly overhangs the exam table, totally obstructing her view of what the doctor was doing.

She'll testify that she was a little light headed from the shot. She'll also tell you that the doctor had been prescribing, on that

day as well as several weeks before, Valium and Tylenol with codeine. She had not taken it that day. Although a little light-headed
from the shot, she was fully cognizant of what was going on around
her. She had seen the doctor tape the sheet up, she could talk, feel
her hands and feet and everything else. And that sheet that had
been taped up to the light overhanging the exam table completely
obstructed her view.

She felt something enter her, enter her vagina, and immediately
said to herself, "This isn't a speculum."

She'll tell you it was unlike anything else any doctor had ever
put inside of her. And she'll tell you that the speculum, when she
had her exams, was cold and hard; it's like steel and it hurts. And
she'll tell you what she felt on March 30 inside her was warm, was
semi-hard, but not hard like steel; and it felt to her — she had had
sex before — it felt like a man's penis.

She'll tell you that when she had pelvic exams before that the
speculum would be put in and opened up, and on this occasion, she
felt something going in and out of her at least four or five times.
And she laid there in astonishment. She could not believe what was
going on; absolutely could not. She could not believe that her doctor of 10 years was raping her in his office.

And she lifted up that sheet to confirm what she thought was
occurring, and as she pulled up that sheet laying on the table, she
lifted her shoulder blades off the table and looked. She saw that
man (indicating Dr. Koo) withdraw his penis from her. And he
turned and she saw his hand move in an upward motion and heard
his pants zip. And before she could move, she saw him grab something off the table next to the examining table, a swab, and put it
inside her, and it was cold. It was wet and it was cold. She'll tell
you she thought it was a cotton swab or some type of gauze. She'll
tell you that she jumped up from the table and she couldn't believe
what happened. And she said to the doctor, "What did you do?
What did you do?"

And he said, "I clean you out."

Before she jumped up from the table after the doctor put the gauze in, he jabbed her with something real sharp and it hurt. And she never had this happen before either. And he told her that it was a boil he popped; and Tammy will tell you that she's had boils before and she knows what they feel like and she didn't have one because she can't wear jeans when she gets them that bad.

And as the doctor is telling her this, she's thinking, "I don't have a boil." And she says, "No, I saw you."

And he says, "No."

And she said, "I saw you, your pants were unzipped."

He goes, "I zip them up; they're zipped."

She goes, "No, you raped me."

At this point Tammy wanted to get out of there, and she got dressed and tried to leave. And the doctor put his hands on her shoulders and said, "Sit down. Sit down." And he proceeded to get an anatomy book, open it up to the portion that had the female genitals, and started showing her that, saying, "No, no, this is what I do."

And he started pointing to things, but Tammy Spasske really couldn't understand what he was saying.

Ladies and gentlemen, she'll tell you that there was no doubt in her mind what she saw. Before she left, the doctor wrote her a prescription for Valium and Tylenol with codeine, the same prescription he had been writing for a long period of time for her.

She went to Walgreen's pharmacy, and she was very upset; she was crying. She asked the pharmacist there, "What do you do when a doctor rapes you?"

She'll tell you she didn't know what to do, she didn't know who to call. She knew that normally you would call a doctor, but what do you do when the doctor does it?

The pharmacist at Walgreen's will tell you that they saw her, that she was emotionally very upset, she was crying, and she asked them, "Is it unusual for someone to get an injection for a pelvic exam?" And that was followed by, "What do you do when a doctor rapes you?"

And they told her that she should call the hospital.

She'll tell you that she went home; she called Munster Hospital — that was close to where she lived — and they said they'd call her back in about an hour. She told them that a doctor had done this. She waited and waited and finally they called to tell her, "Call the police. Go to the Hammond Clinic."

She called the police and an officer came out to her house. He'll testify that he talked to her and said she had to go get an assault kit done and said she should go to the Hammond Clinic or St. Margaret's Hospital. So she went to the clinic because it was close to home, but the clinic didn't do assault kits, so she went to St. Margaret's.

There the nurse took the sexual assault test and that consists of attempting to collect any seminal fluid that might be in the victim's vagina, collecting hairs from her head and from her pubic area — hairs that are pulled out, not cut, to include the root. Her underwear was taken to be tested for traces of seminal fluid, and she had to sit there. She'll tell you how degrading it was.

At the hospital she was contacted by a person from Haven House, a rape counseling center, and then entered therapy for rape counseling.

Ladies and gentlemen, you will hear testimony from Lisa Black from the Indiana State Police Lab and Kim Epperson, also from the Indiana State Police Lab.

Ms. Black, a hair specialist, does hair comparisons that can match up a hair to a certain race or a certain individual. She will testify that in only about four percent of the cases of sexual contact, consensual or non-consensual, is there a transfer of pubic hair. In this case there was no transfer of pubic hair, which is a normal finding.

Ms. Epperson will tell you how they test for the presence of any seminal fluid in a rape kit. She will tell you that she examined the sample from a swab of Tammy Spasske's vaginal area, first testing for the presence of acid phosphate, an enzyme secreted from the prostate gland of the male during sex. She'll tell you one of the preliminary tests was positive for acid phosphate, and when that happens testing is then done for sperm cells and something called P-30 — all components of male ejaculation.

She'll tell you that the tests were negative for sperm and for P-30, but she'll also tell you that the presence of acid phosphate and the lack of sperm and P-30 is totally consistent with someone who is cleaned out with some type of alcohol or peroxide that would kill sperm cells and the P-30, but not get rid of the acid phosphate. She'll tell you that's consistent with the passage of time — in this case several hours passed before the test was made. She'll also tell you it's totally consistent with sexual intercourse in which there is no ejaculation, because acid phosphate is contained in the pree-jaculation fluid.

Tammy Spasske will tell you that the doctor did not ejaculate inside her.

Ms. Epperson will also tell you that acid phosphate can be present from vaginal bleeding, but in this case there wasn't any vaginal blood present in the sample she tested. She will also tell you these results might be consistent with a yeast infection.

Ladies and gentlemen, that's the testimony you will hear. During the voir dire process I asked that if the State proved its case beyond reasonable doubt if you could return a verdict of guilty. Well, I believe the evidence will show that on March 30, 1989, on Kennedy Avenue in Hammond, Indiana, that man raped Tammy Spasske when she was unaware that it was occurring, unaware until she looked under that sheet and saw him pull out of her.

I'm going to ask you during this trial to keep in mind your life's experiences and common sense, and I believe that you will find the defendant guilty of raping Tammy Spasske when she was unaware of it.

Thank you very much.

* * *

DEFENSE ATTORNEY BRECLAW'S OPENING STATEMENT

The beauty of our jury system — and you are the most important people in this courtroom, not Dr. Koo, not the judge, because in your hands, you hold the Constitutional form of government which dictates that each defendant, each citizen is presumed innocent in a court of law until the evidence proves beyond a reasonable doubt the crime as charged. You are the most important people in this courtroom.

Normally in a burglary you have a building that is broken into; in a homicide you have a dead body; but in this case you have basically the assertions of a woman. And these assertions are fears that every professional man has when he is dealing in his office with a client or patient of the opposite sex.

Is this the product of this woman's imagination? To a physician who has lovingly treated his patient for 10 years, and you will hear testimony of this treatment to her, and she will tell you that never in 10 years had he been suggestive to her in a sexual way, and always he has treated her with professional care and consideration. Through 10 years of extensive medical problems that deal not only with the bumps and scrapes of life, but with a complicated medical problem that deals with female problems of a bloating stomach, cramping, pains, vaginal discharges that extend back to the birth of her daughter some eight or nine years prior to that. You have to ask yourself why on March 30 does this loving physician assault this woman.

Mr. Benson indicated to you in his fine opening statement that you are to use common sense and human experience, and I would also ask you on behalf of Doctor Koo to use those two factors. Ladies and gentlemen, things just don't make sense in this case.

Where did this happen?

* * *

The Court permitted Mr. Breclaw to display a drawing of Dr. Koo's Kennedy Avenue office (see Figure 2).

* * *

It happens at the doctor's office, which has been there for a number of years on Kennedy Avenue across from Freddie's Steak House. And the office will become an important consideration in this case. As you walk in, there is a reception area where patients sit. There is a window here where the receptionist sits; it's a reception office for appointments, payments, and the like. From the reception area a door opens into a long hallway that runs east and west. The first door to the right is to the reception office, the second to examining room number one.

Now, this examining room is somewhat unique because there's a sliding door that connects with the reception office, and that will become important.

The next door leads to examining room number two, the same size room, but there is no sliding door into the other examining room.

Now a patient in examining room number one on the examining table would have her head to the north and her feet to the south. These doors have no locks on them; there are no locks.

Secondly, this examining table is fixed; it's not adjustable; it doesn't move up and down. In the corners are the trays that Doctor uses to contain his K-Y jelly. This is a jelly that is used to facilitate a bimanual examination of the vagina, which I will explain later, or to ease insertion of the speculum. Also in this room is a goose-

Figure 1. Dr. Koo's Office

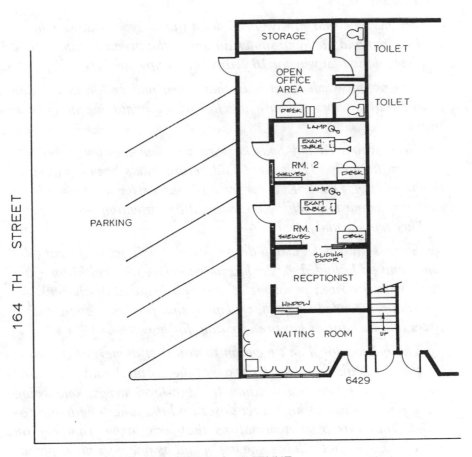

neck lamp; this is a lamp with a light and you can move it around. This is what the doctor, after he drapes the patient, tapes the sheet to. By the way, for 10 years, he's been doing the same thing with Tammy Spasske. This prevents the sheet from falling between the legs of the female, which then prevents the doctor from seeing the vaginal area and taking his specimens through the speculum for the Pap smear test.

So the sheet has always been done that way; it's always taped to the lamp and the lamp shines a light in the area of examination. It's been done that way for 10 years; that's how he does it.

I think the wash basin is in that room and cotton swabs and things that doctors will use in clinical examinations in general practice.

Now, who's Tammy Spasske? She is a woman now in her late twenties (actually 31), and as I said before, she's been a patient of this physician, Doctor Koo, for over 10 years. Her whole family, in fact, has come to Doctor Koo for medical attention — her sister and her mother and father.

She also has been taking drugs, which I will get into a little bit later, and as I alluded to, she has an extensive medical history that deals with a host of problems of stomach, vaginal discharges, severe pain, extended stomach, cramping that has been going on for years that this doctor has been treating for her.

The prosecutor didn't mention to you that as part of this rape kit, there was also a urinalysis taken at the hospital, and in this urinalysis, they found two medium to high-level drugs, one being Valium in medium to high-level doses and the other one being codeine. This was from a urinalysis that was taken from her on March 30, and that will become important as one possible explanation of what had occurred.

And by the way, I'm only offering possible explanations because I really don't know. The point is, with the presumption of innocence, the State must prove beyond a reasonable doubt that there was a rape. I don't have to explain or prove that there wasn't. But part of my presentation will be trying to find some explanation of how this could have happened.

Now, I was able to obtain her prescription records, and interestingly enough, this is what I found with respect to Valium. She was taking Valium and this is a drug that affects the central nervous system, and according to the Physicians Desk Book Reference, one of the side effects is hallucination and drowsiness. Doctor Sabelli, a pharmacologist and psychiatrist, will testify that together with codeine Valium is very effective in producing hallucinations — or can produce an hallucination with a sexual fantasy. He will talk about situationally produced fantasies, but I'll go into that a little later.

These are drugs that came from Fairmeadows Pharmacy in Munster. They deliver to your house; you call up and they deliver it. But that also caused a problem.

On February 17, 1989 there was a new prescription. I think she was given 60 tablets for a 15 day supply. But she doesn't use that new prescription; she renews an older one by calling up on the phone.

On February 27 she renews it — that's what the "R" is, 60 tablets, 15-day supply. That's roughly four a day. She then waits 14 days and renews it again on March 13 at Fairmeadows Pharmacy, 60 tablets for 15 days.

Now, this is also the date that she goes in, I believe, to see Doctor Koo the first time in March. She then on March 20 goes in and gets 60 tablets more; that's only a week later, which is a 15 day supply.

So within seven days she is ostensibly renewing this prescription; and if she's taking those tablets she is doing a double dose. Now, on March 27 that's another seven days, she renews the prescription again for Valium, gets 60 more tablets, and there's only

been a lapse of seven days. Now, if she's taking these, she's dou-
bling up on them.

Now, from March 27 until March 30, Doctor writes her a new
prescription on March 30 which she takes to Walgreen's and she
gets refilled after she leaves his office. She gets a new prescription
from him after just having filled a refill three days before that.
Now, you have this woman — if she's taking this stuff — on a
three-day interval, that means she is now taking 20 a day. Now, she
has testified in a deposition and she'll testify here that no one else
was taking them in her house; she wasn't giving them to anybody;
she wasn't selling them to anybody. But she told me under oath
that she took one a night to go to sleep. possibly two. I think very
rarely she took three.

And that's under oath. Fairmeadows has a policy when they get
a prescription they just refill it automatically five times, so I suspect it was from one that was obtained prior to February 17. At the
same time she's also taking codeine, and codeine, the testimony
will be, is a mind-altering drug. Hallucinations are a side effect of
it. In conjunction with other drugs there is, according to Doctor
Sabelli, a potentiation — a boosting effect greater than the combined effect of the two drugs. For example, if the effect of codeine
is two and the effect of Valium is two, the combined effect might be
greater than four — eight or 10 even. So you have two controlled
substances that she is taking, hallucinating potentiality in these
drugs, and, again, with the codeine, she is filling these ahead of
schedule. Three pharmacies she is getting this at — Walgreen's,
Highland and Fairmeadows.

MR. BENSON   "Objection, Your Honor. I don't believe there
is any evidence she ever picked up any of these, that they were prescriptions that were written and filled, and that it's argumentative
whether or not she picked them up ever. ''

MR. BRECLAW   "Well, they were delivered or someone
picked them up.''

THE COURT   "Ladies and gentlemen of the jury, you're simply reminded that what the lawyers are telling you is what they expect their evidence will show. I'm going to be asking you to do something that is not always easy, but it is a part of your duty so I would assume you would do it. And that is despite what might be said during these opening statements by either the State or the defense, if evidence is not produced during the trial to establish these things, you must disregard what has been said in opening statements; it is not a fact on which you can base your verdict."

* * *

Mr. Breclaw continued to present, item by item, the records of numerous prescriptions that he claimed were filled for Tammy Spasske. He suggested to the jury that she actually picked up and took a very large number of tablets — codeine and Valium — because he had a written record that three pharmacies filled them over the time indicated.

* * *

I think we have to go back to February 24, approximately a month before. She had been in Doctor's office complaining of an injury that she received to her right breast — a shortness of breath. And Doctor at that time gave her a shot of pain medication, xylocaine, and a prescription for Valium and empirin with codeine number IV. Tammy Spasske came into this office on February 24, and this was for an injury she had received to the breast area, and he treated that injury with medication and then sent her on her way. And there are some significant dates in this case, the first being February 24. This is the first date I think relevant to this whole scenario. She will testify that she also was suffering from her usual pelvic pains, extended stomach, but it was something that she could live with apparently because that wasn't a major complaint on that date.

The next time Doctor sees her is on March 14, and at this time she came into his office with complaints of swelling in her stomach area, pain I think she will describe as bad pain, and discharge. Hearing her complaints and knowing her history, he did a pelvic examination.

The exam protocol consists of a number of things; one is a breast examination done in the doctor's office. A Doctor Black, family practitioner from Valparaiso, will testify that the standard of care is not to have a third party present unless requested by the patient.

The second part of the examination involves a disrobing from the waist down with the patient given a paper modesty sheet. Tammy Spasske will testify the sheet was placed around her waist area.

After the feet are placed in the stirrups and the legs are spread apart so the doctor can view the area, the testimony will be that he tapes the sheet onto the lamp in order to give him a clear view of the examination area. With the light on he makes a visual examination and then applies what we call K-Y jelly for lubrication on the lips, labia of the vagina, inside the vagina, and on the speculum. This is done to ease placement of the speculum and subsequent bimanual examination. The doctor must open up the vagina to see inside and to take samples swabbed from the cervix to be sent to a lab — it's a Pap smear for early detection of cancer.

After that part of the examination is completed, the speculum is then removed and the doctor will do a palpitation of the vaginal lips, just a feeling around the vagina for any abnormal growth or warts.

He wears gloves, and these gloves are cream-colored, sort of like cream color, brown. You've seen them, surgical gloves. And after he has felt the outer lips of the vagina, he then inserts his fingers into the vagina while standing up pressing against the top of the woman's stomach and moving his fingers back and forth. He's trying to feel the female anatomy for purposes of any enlargement or displacement, and he is against the woman as her legs are spread, and he's pushing in with his fingers, feeling on the right side, feeling in the middle, feeling on the left and moving his hand in and out during the bimanual examination. Then he withdraws his hand and grabs gauze which he uses to clean up the female, clean up the K-Y jelly.

She will testify that she was in extreme pain and it's not unusual for him to give her a shot when she's being treated during an examination for pain or other problems. She will tell you he normally gives the shot in the buttocks area rather than the arm.

If he did inject her with Valium, as she will testify he told her, testimony from Dr. Sabelli will be that Valium is used as an anesthetic for minor procedures and some invasive procedures. A doctor will say that Valium has been very suspect in the last few years and possibly is not the drug of choice. But regardless, she will say that she heard him say Valium.

So that is what he does with her based upon her complaints. He does a clinical examination, which he calls a pelvic exam, on March 14, 1989.

He then prescribes prescriptions for discharge, a moist massage for the breast, and a suppository, and tells her to continue the medication that he gave her in February.

She comes back on March 28 with complaints of a distended stomach, pain and swelling. He takes her into the examining room and does not have her disrobe. He has her unzip her slacks and he presses down on the stomach area and tells her he's going to need an x-ray. She wants a mammogram as well and he writes a prescription for both and she leaves his office.

I might add, backtracking to March 14, that she went home and told her mother that something didn't feel right with the doctor, like playing with the lips of her vagina. And her mother told her it was her imagination, that the doctor had been their trusted family physician for over 10 years. Her mother will testify to this and to her concern about the way he examined her breasts.

Then, on March 30, she went back to the doctor. Now, Doctor Sabelli will talk about a situationally-induced hallucination. And what is that? It's a hallucination that occurs because the situation reminds you of another situation. In this case she will state, I suspect, that she was apprehensive about what was to be happening to her, that this situation on March 30 fell back to what she felt had happened on March 14.

Now Doctor Sabelli will testify that with situationally-induced hallucinations, you see this quite common in dental chairs, people who are under anesthetic for teeth extractions where there are hallucinations because of the mouth area and of the mouth cavity, and these particular hallucinations have basically dealt with oral sex because of the situation as it is involved. So on March 30 she returns to the Doctor in pain again and to find out about the x-ray results. She will tell you she went to examining room number two, the farthest examining room from the reception area.

Now, in the office, there was nobody there, she said, except the receptionist. In her statement of April 3, 1989 she states that doctor left the room, she undressed, and he came in through the sliding doors as he always does.

You will see from the evidence these doors close. There is only one sliding door that separates the receptionist, the closest door to examining room number one. I think the evidence will show that she was, in fact, in examining room number one right next door to the receptionist. These doors are without locks as I have mentioned.

She will testify that Doctor gave her the shot of Valium, that he prepped her for an examination, and that he draped the sheet in the usual manner above the light, and then she notices she doesn't feel the cold speculum.

I asked her during that examination — and I suspect she'll testify — to describe this thing that she saw coming out of her vagina.

And I anticipate her testimony concerning the penis would be like this.

"When you saw this, was it a glimpse of the entire penis, a portion of the penis?" Answer, "It was — I'm not really sure. I know it was attached to his body; I saw it for just a brief second." "Did you see the head or tip of the penis, or are we talking about the root or where it starts that you saw?" Answer, "I'm not really sure. It was too quick to tell, but I know what it was; I mean I could describe it." "So it was a brief glimpse. And what you're telling me is that I could ask you a lot of dumb questions about the penis but you wouldn't be able to get me much of a description; is that a fair statement?" Answer, "Yes, sir."

That's what I anticipate her testimony would be concerning the penis.

From her statement she is drowsy from the drug that she had received and she said to him, "What did you just do?" And he said, "I clean you up," which is a normal part of a pelvic examination. She says, "No, your pants, your zipper," and he said, "My pants are zipped."

She sees him zip up the zipper the same time he's reaching for gauze and she's looking at his side. His right hand, the zipper, the left hand reaching for the gauze.

Now, from the two statements she gave to the police and will testify here, I would ask her, "Did he turn his back to you?" and she would answer, "No, he just turned to the side. And he grabbed the Q-tip thing and it was wet and it was long and wooden and it had cotton on the end and he put it inside me. And as he was doing that, I saw him zip his zipper." No where in the two statements that she gave police does she mention hearing the zipper. No where in the extensive deposition she gave me does she mention that. The first time I heard it was today from Mr. Benson.

I will ask her, "And he picked up the Q-tip type device?" And she will answer, "Yeah, and he zipped his pants with the right

hand." "And you're saying his pants were unzipped at that time?"
Answer, "Yes." Question, "Was his penis still visible?" Answer,
"no." "Did he zip himself up afterwards? Answer, "It's hard to
think. I'm really not sure. If it wasn't exactly at the same time, then
it was like a second later."

She will testify that he gets an anatomy book and starts show-
ing her the organs of the female and trying to explain what her
problem is; he takes the time to do that. He still doesn't compre-
hend at that point, I believe.

She will testify she's in shock, then leaves and goes to the Wal-
green's. By the way, he writes prescriptions for her after explain-
ing what her problems are — an antibiotic, Tylenol and another
Valium. He is not aware that she is getting Valium refills.

She goes home and eventually to the hospital where they do the
sexual assault kit or rape kit. Now specimens from inside the va-
gina sent to the State Police Lab showed no evidence of sperm. I
think she'll testify he didn't have time to ejaculate inside of her or
she doesn't think that he ejaculated inside of her. Then they take a
pubic hair count to see if there is a foreign hair. In this case there
were Caucasian pubic hairs and not Mongoloid as you would find
from a man of Korean origin.

So there's no physical evidence in this case of any sperm or pu-
bic hairs. Then they run a urine test on her and find medium to
high levels of Valium and codeine.

This doctor, by the way, did call Tammy's father and met with
him the next day. He was very concerned about the allegations and
the girl. And then, for the next 21 months nothing happens. He con-
tinued on with his life until January of 1991 when he is ordered to
turn over this woman's medical records to the prosecutor. State-
ments are taken of various witnesses and then he's arrested and
he's charged with rape. And I get into the case at that point when
he calls me.

I'm sure Tammy Spasske will testify that she was mad and had called the prosecutor's office (about the 21-month delay). She will say she became somewhat of a rape activist and wanted to go on Oprah Winfrey's show and was told by Detective Burczyk that that wouldn't be a smart thing to do.

She stated she'd been to Haven House where battered women are handled. She will testify that she was told by a counselor there she has to go through with this (trial).

And on the last day — the last day you can file a civil suit, two years after incident took place — she filed a civil suit looking for money damages.

Why did this happen? I don't know the intricacies of the human mind and the motivations. Was it a hallucination? Was it her imagination clouded by drugs? Was it an apprehension? Is she an activist now? Is it the law suit for monetary gain? Is it a bitterness she now holds against him for some reason, for some unknown reason? Or is it a combination of these?

Regardless, he has the presumption of innocence, and it is upon the State to prove beyond a reasonable doubt that this man raped this woman.

This is not a case of a woman who goes to a doctor on her first or second visit complaining of a sore throat and finds herself disrobed on an examining table for a pelvic examination. This woman received kind, considerate, competent medical care from her family physician, Doctor Koo.

At the conclusion of this case, I will ask you to return a verdict of not guilty.

Thank you.

* * *

When the judge instructed Mr. Benson to present evidence on behalf of the State, the young prosecutor announced that the State would call Ms. Tammy Spasske Garza to the witness stand. Not only the eyes of every juror, but also the eyes of every person in the courtroom turned toward the first witness for the prosecution as she entered the court and walked slowly toward the witness stand.

2
Accusation by Tammy

July 14 • Tuesday • early afternoon

She was tall, blonde, and slender. Her beauty was of that ethereal quality so hard to describe. There was a haunting look about her, coupled with a touch of hardness, or perhaps strength.

I guess the two-piece tailored business suit with its double breasted jacket and just-below-the-knee length skirt was as appropriate as could be expected. It did look a bit out of place on her, as if purchased for the occasion, never to be worn again.

She took her seat at the witness stand and, ever so slowly, turned her face toward the jury — as though she wanted a close look at the people who would sit in judgment of her charge of rape. There was little or no makeup to hide the obvious strain of the past three years. She reminded me of a cornered animal braced for a final fight to the death. You could sense her fear; you could sense her resolve.

She gave her present name as Tammy Jane Garza, her married name. She was not married back in 1989 and, at that time, went by her maiden name — Tammy Spasske.

In response to Benson's questioning she gave her age as 31 and indicated that her husband of less than one year was present in the courtroom. Her only child was a girl of 10. While unemployed at the time of the alleged rape, she had been working at Kmart since September of 1991. She then identified the defendant as Dr. Koo, her physician for 11 years prior to 1989.

He was also treating her parents, her sisters, and her brother — having taken over the practice of the family's former physician.

It was shortly after her daughter was born in 1982 that she began having vaginal problems — bleeding, pains in the stomach and bloating. While under the care of Dr. Koo, she underwent a D & C three times and a laparoscopy twice in an effort to bring her back to good health. Tammy explained the D & C as a dilation (swelling and expanding) and curettage (surgical cleaning and scraping) of the uterus, and the laparotomy as a surgical sectioning of the abdominal wall for diagnosis.

She testified that for about two years prior to March 1989 she had been taking Valium and some form of codeine (Tylenol with codeine number IV or empirin with codeine number IV) as prescribed by Dr. Koo for relief of anxiety and pain respectively.

State Attorney Benson then introduced a diagram of Dr. Koo's office on Kennedy Avenue and identified it as State's Exhibit Number 1 (see Figure 2).

Tammy recognized the diagram as Dr. Koo's office and went on to describe the doors from the hallway to both examination rooms as sliding. When asked about the door from the reception area to examination room number one, Tammy vaguely remembered it as sliding also.

Testifying to undergoing over 50 pelvic exams from Dr. Koo, she added, "To the best of my recollection there was always a receptionist in her office when I went in for an exam. I would go to either examination room where I would undress from the waist down. The doctor usually stepped out when I undressed. He would hand me the paper sheet, tell me to undress, and leave the room until I was ready. Then he would come back in."

Mr. Benson, with Defense Attorney Breclaw's agreement, then marked as State's Exhibit Number 2 the paper sheet that Mr. Breclaw had used for demonstration during his opening statement. Tammy indicated that it was similar in size, shape, and material to those she had described.

She told of her March 14 visit to Dr. Koo because of pelvic problems — pain, bloating, bleeding. She remembered being directed to examining room number two where she undressed and wrapped the paper sheet around her waist.

As she stepped away from the witness stand to demonstrate to the jury how the paper sheet was wrapped, Judge Page directed that in the future that item would be called a "paper drape."

While waiting for the doctor to return, Tammy sat on the side of the exam table with the paper drape in place. The table itself was standard — stirrups for the feet that extended from both sides of one end, a step that could be pulled out from the bottom on that end, and storage drawers along one side.

Tammy's testimony then confirmed the essential details of Dr. Koo's examination on March 14 that Mr. Benson had covered in his opening statement — including her perception of the doctor's fingers moving around the lips of her vagina and the concern she expressed to her mother.

She added that Dr. Koo told her she had a vaginal infection and that he prescribed Monistat 7, a vaginal cream for yeast infections, and gave her hydrocodone — telling her to return in two weeks if she wasn't feeling better.

Asked about anything else on March 14 she said, "Well, he examined my breast. About a month and a half before, my ex-boyfriend had beat me up and he had hit me in my right breast and there was still hardness there, and the doctor just told me that I would have to use heat on it."

Her testimony then confirmed Mr. Benson's opening statement concerning the events of March 28 and the doctor's order for x-rays of her stomach and breast.

When she called Dr. Koo's office at 2:00 p.m. on March 30 he told her she had cysts on her ovaries and an infection in her fallopian tubes. His receptionist told her to come in before 3:00 that afternoon. Tammy drove herself in her father's car to the doctor's office. Only the doctor and his receptionist were present.

She testified to being sent to examination room number two and told by the doctor to undress for a pelvic examination. By 3:00 p.m. on March 30, 1989, Tammy Spasske was seated on the side of the exam table, undressed below the waist with a paper drape in place about her.

* * *

MR. BENSON

    Q.   Where were you seated?''

TAMMY

    A.   "I was on the exam table. I wasn't laying down; I was sitting on it like sideways with my feet hanging down.''

    Q.   "Had he discussed anything about what he was going to do?''

    A.   "No, sir.''

    Q.   "And when he walked in, what happened?''

    A.   "He grabbed my right arm and gave me an injection.''

    Q.   "Did you say anything to him about that?''

    A.   "I said, 'What was that?' And he said, 'Make you feel good.' And I go, 'Well, what's in it?' And he says, 'Valium.' ''

Q.   "Had he ever given you a shot before a pelvic exam on any other occasion?"

A.   "Before the exam, no."

Q.   "Had he ever given you shots after a pelvic exam?"

A.   "Yes, as a matter of fact, on March 28 when I was in there, after I was done — I forgot — he gave me a shot for pain."

Q.   "Where was that shot given to you at?"

A.   "In the buttocks area, hip."

Q.   "And all the time you went to Doctor Koo, had you ever received an injection in the arm?"

A.   "No, sir, always in the buttocks area. He had you loosen your pants a little and he just gave you a shot there. This was the first time I ever had one by Doctor Koo in the arm."

Q.   "And there was no one else in the room, was there?"

A.   "No, sir."

Q.   "And there was no one else in the office, correct?"

A.   "The receptionist was there."

Q.   "Other than that?"

A.   "Oh, no."

Q.   "So the doctor knew that you had not come down there with anyone, correct?"

A.   "Yes."

Q.   "There was no one in the waiting area?"

A.   "No."

Q.   "What happened after you received the injection?"

A.   "He told me to scoot to the end of the table."

Q.   "And where was the paper drape?"

A.   "Well, it was around my waist, and then when I scooted
       down, he took the paper drape and he taped it to the over-
       hanging lamp, as always."

Q.   "The corner of it?"

A.   The corner of it."

Q.   Could you see the doctor then?"

A.   No."

Q.   Now, when you first came in and were waiting for the
       doctor, did you see the speculum on the table where it
       normally was positioned?"

A.   "Not that day, no."

Q.   "Did you see anything on the table?"

A.   "I think there was gauze and stuff, Q-tips."

Q.   "Now, at any time, had the doctor told you what he was
       going to do?"

A.   "No."

Q.   "You thought you were going to get a pelvic exam, cor-
       rect?"

A.   "Yes."

Q.   "Now, did this shot have any effect on you?"

A.   "I felt a little light headed."

Q.   "Could you still see?"

A.   "Yes."

Q.   "Was any part of your body numb?

A.   "No, sir.

Q.   "Could you talk?

A.   "Yes.

Q.   "Other than being light headed, was there any other ef-
       fect?

A.   "No."

Q.   "And what happened as you were sitting on the exam table with your feet in the stirrups?"

A.   "I felt something go inside me, and it wasn't the speculum."

Q.   "Now, what was inside you, how did it differ from a speculum?"

A.   "The speculum is always hard and steel and always cold; this wasn't cold; it wasn't hard and it didn't hurt. The speculum always hurts when it first goes in because of the steel. This wasn't like that at all. I've never felt that in any of the exams I've had before by Doctor Koo."

Q.   "And what, if anything, did you feel when you felt this object enter you?"

A.   [Witness crying] "I don't want to stop. I felt tickling in and out of me and in and out, and I also felt his body pressing back and forth against my upper thigh area on the back part right below my buttocks."

Q.   "Where were his hands?"

A.   "His hands were on both sides of my legs, the lower part, through here [indicating]."

Q.   "And what part of his body did you feel hitting your inside thighs?"

A.   "The front part of his legs."

Q.   "Is there any doubt in your mind as to whether or not you felt one or two of his hands on your body when this occurred?"

A.   "Both of them were there. I could feel one of them on each leg part."

Q.   "Approximately how long did this continue for?"

A.   "It seemed like forever but I think it was only a couple of minutes."

Q.   "And what were you thinking during this time?"

A.   "I didn't know what to think. I couldn't believe what was going on."

Q.   "What did you do?"

A.   "I wanted to be sure. I knew what was going on but I just wanted to be sure, and I lifted the end of the sheet that was in front of me and I looked under and I saw Doctor Koo's penis and I saw it pull out of me."

Q.   "You're absolutely sure that's what you saw?"

A.   "Positive. It was —"

MR. BRECLAW   "Objection. Counsel is testifying."

THE COURT   "Overruled."

MR. BENSON

Q.   "What was your answer?"

TAMMY

A.   "Positive. It was attached to his body."

Q.   "And what did you see happen next?"

A.   "I saw his penis pull out of me and then he turned to the right, his right towards the table where the little exam tray is next to him. Then he grabbed something off the table. It was — I don't know. It was like a Q-tip; it looked like a Q-tip but it was long and skinny and wooden and it had either gauze or cotton on the end of it. And as he turned, I saw him zip his zipper. And then he came back with the Q-tip and he put it inside me and it was wet and it was cold."

Q.   "At any time you felt the defendant's penis inside of you, did he ejaculate?"

A.   "No, he couldn't have had time."

Q.   "Now, after you saw the defendant remove his penis from you, put the swab inside you, what, if anything, did you do or say?"

A.   "Then I didn't say anything. I saw him zip his zipper. I don't know what it was, but he poked me with something sharp and I jumped up and off the table and I asked him, I said, 'What did you do?' And he said, 'I popped a boil.' "

* * *

There now arose the risk of the jury hearing testimony not permitted under the rules of evidence. Tammy might inadvertently blurt out something said by Doctor Koo that could be considered hearsay, and thus inadmissible as evidence. The prosecution wanted to present the doctor's statement as evidence allowed under the *res gestae* exception which allows the admission of words spoken spontaneously and concurrently with an incident. The defense did not want the jury to hear the doctor's statement.

* * *

MR. BRECLAW   "May we approach the bench, Your Honor?"

THE COURT   "You may approach the bench."

WHEREUPON THE FOLLOWING DISCUSSION WAS HELD AT THE BENCH OUTSIDE OF THE HEARING OF THE JURY:

MR. BRECLAW   "Your Honor, we're getting into the area of something that has been a subject of a Motion in Limine and I would like the witness instructed not to testify as to what comments Doctor may have made."

THE COURT   "Has she been instructed in that regard?"

MR. BENSON "Yes, and at this time, I'm going to ask the Court to hear that testimony. I believe it's relevant, maybe not through the opening statement, but at this point, Your Honor. We contend it's part of the *res gestae* and it's a statement made immediately after this incident, within two or three minutes."

THE COURT "Mr. Breclaw?"

MR. BRECLAW "Your Honor, the statement is made after a couple other things happened. One where she accuses him about the zipper and sounds about a zipper and then she asked him about what he's doing and he says, 'Cleaning you up.' The act in question is the penis and the vagina, and what he said at that particular time. Now we're getting into facts where she's accusing him and asking for explanations and it's our position that this is evidence of other acts that is coming in past the time of *res gestae,* past the time of the intercourse."

THE COURT "We're a little bit ahead of ourselves. Let's reach this point before we do it. We're at other questions first."

MR. BENSON "We're probably within four questions, Your Honor."

THE COURT "Well, that's four questions from now."

WHEREUPON THE FOLLOWING PROCEEDINGS WERE ONCE AGAIN HELD IN THE HEARING OF THE JURY:

MR. BENSON:

Q.   "You said you asked the doctor what did he do?"

TAMMY

A.   "Yes, sir."

Q.   "Were you still on the exam table at that time?"

A.   "I jumped up and off it. No, I was standing."

Q.   "And did the doctor tell you what he did?"

A.   "He said, 'I popped a boil.' "

Q.   "What did you say?"

A.   "I said, 'No, what did you do?' I was yelling at him. And then he said, 'I clean you out.' "

Q.   "What did you do next?"

MR. BRECLAW "May we approach the bench, Your Honor?"

THE COURT "You may approach the bench."

WHEREUPON THE FOLLOWING DISCUSSION WAS HELD AT THE BENCH OUTSIDE OF THE HEARING OF THE JURY:

MR. BRECLAW "There are some long pauses in her answers now, indicating that she's probably at the point where she's being forced to talk about the accusation of 'this happened before.' So I mean there are other issues involved, that she dresses up first, that he claimed the zipper was zipped."

THE COURT "Would you prefer to have Mr. Benson lead?"

MR. BRECLAW "At this point, yes."

THE COURT Mr. Benson, you will lead."

WHEREUPON THE FOLLOWING PROCEEDINGS WERE ONCE AGAIN HELD IN THE HEARING OF THE JURY:

MR. BENSON:

Q.   "Did there come a point where you got off the table?"

TAMM

A.   "Yes."

Q.   "And did you get dressed immediately or was there some time span between you getting of the table and you starting to get dressed?"

A.   "I just jumped up and off it and I was just standing there for a minute and that's when the conversation took place."

Q.   "What did the doctor do? Not what he said, but what did he do after you jumped off the table?"

A.   "He just stood there."

Q.   "You had a conversation with the doctor about his zipper?"

A.   "I asked him why did he zip his zipper and he motioned to his pants with his hand like that [indicating], and he said, 'They're zipped.' And I said, 'Yeah, I just saw you zip them.' "

Q.   "What did he say in return?"

A."   "Nothing."

Q.   "What, if anything, happened after that?"

A.   "I was getting dressed then and he sort of motioned me with his — put his hands like on my shoulder and like sort of guided me to the chair and sat me down. It wasn't forceful or anything, just like guided."

Q.   "What did he do at that point?"

A."   "He was writing out a prescription."

Q.   "How much time elapsed from the time that you argued with him about the zipper until the time he started writing the prescription?

A.   "It wasn't all that long."

Q.   "A couple of seconds?"

A.   "Yeah, roughly. It was less than a minute."

MR. BENSON   "Judge, I would ask permission to approach at this point."

THE COURT   "You may approach."

WHEREUPON THE FOLLOWING DISCUSSION WAS HELD AT THE BENCH OUTSIDE OF THE HEARING OF THE JURY:

MR. BENSON   "We're there."

THE COURT   "Are you telling me that the entire conversation between her and the doctor has now been exhausted and every detail of what he said to her and everything of what she said to him has been related?"

MR. BENSON   "The only thing left for her to say is that he pulled out a book."

THE COURT   "Let's get through that first. We're dealing with millisecond by millisecond."

MR. BENSON   It's as he's pulling out the book that he says, 'I need a nurse in here. This happened to me before.' It's all simultaneous."

THE COURT   "You made a statement during opening statement that she accused him of raping her. Now, did you overstate yourself? Because that's the first time I've heard that she said that to him."

MR. BENSON   "She said that she saw his penis."

THE COURT   "Did she say that out loud to him?"

MR. BENSON   "To him, she said, "I saw it."

THE COURT   "Now, I want you to lay a solid foundation of what was said between the two of them. Cover every word of what was said between the two of them. I need to know what was said before I can intelligently rule on it. What is then supposed to have been said to the nurse?"

MR. BENSON   "He didn't say anything to the nurse; there was a statement about a nurse."

THE COURT   Oh, he didn't say that out the door?"

MR. BENSON   "No, he said that to her. It's coming up right now, 'This happened to me before.' "

THE COURT   "I haven't heard the discussion about the books."

MR. BENSON   "It happens as he's getting the book. It was right there."

THE COURT   "Mr. Breclaw?"

MR. BRECLAW   "It's my understanding that this entire communication between the two includes she has not made an accusation of him that he has had intercourse with her. She's asking him what he was doing, he's responding, 'I'm cleaning you out.' She's off the table. He is at this point stating that his zipper is zipped; he's sitting down; he has guided her to another part of the room; sat her down. He's writing her prescription, and now he's about to get up and get an anatomy book."

THE COURT   "Okay, and that's when he said what he's supposed to have said?"

MR. BRECLAW   "That would be my understanding of what is coming up. And then he will say, 'I need a nurse in here. This happened before.' "

MR. BENSON   "Her testimony is within minutes, and *res gestae* exceptions have been extended to hours."

THE COURT   "Well, you're dealing with a different issue than *res gestae* here."

MR. BENSON   "We believe this is admissible to show his state of mind, because he denied it, and he knows he should have someone in there but he didn't because his motive was to do this, to have this rape."

THE COURT   "Are you telling me that this is the next thing that is said?"

MR. BENSON   "Well, as he's getting the books, I believe she's going to say, 'He was getting the books when he said — ' "

THE COURT   "And then he began to explain to her what — see, you haven't covered that yet."

MR. BENSON   "Well, it's going to blurt out, Your Honor."

BY THE COURT   "I want the sequence exactly. We're dealing with a very specific sequence of statements going back and
forth between the two over a period of several minutes. Exactly
what was said makes a difference. I would like to have that firmly
established.

MR. BRECLAW   "Your Honor, his leading this witness, really leading this witness, I have no objection to that."

THE COURT   "All right, I'll explain to the jury how the
prosecutor is going to lead."

WHEREUPON THE FOLLOWING PROCEEDINGS WERE
ONCE AGAIN HELD IN THE HEARING OF THE JURY:

THE COURT   "Ladies and gentlemen of the jury, to avoid
certain hearsay problems — and you may have heard that term before, and I'll explain it if it comes up — it's necessary for either
side during their questioning to lay what is called the foundation.
They have to ask certain questions in a very particular way in order
to lay a foundation before certain other questions can be asked.
What you see here is we're going over that. Mr. Benson has been
instructed to lay his foundation. In order to do so, he must what we
call lead the witness. We don't normally do that; we don't normally
allow somebody who brings a witness in to lead that witness. We
don't allow them by their question to suggest what the answer
might be. But so that Mr. Benson lays his foundation properly, he
will be permitted to ask leading questions. We don't want that in
any way to be misunderstood as Mr. Benson putting words in the
witness's mouth. So, Mr. Benson, you may lead the witness."

MR. BENSON   "Thank you, Judge."

Q.   "Ms. Tammy, you testified that the doctor took you by
       the shoulders and sat you down in the chair and got an
       anatomy book, correct?"

A.   "Yes."

Q.   "And he opened that anatomy book to certain pages of the female genital organs, correct?"

A.   "The female anatomy, yes."

Q.   "And did he tell you — start to show you and tell you that you had some kind of infection down there?"

A.   "To the best of my knowledge, yes."

Q.   "And he started to write out prescriptions?"

A.   "Yes."

Q.   "Do you recall how many?"

A.   "There — no. I think it was Valium, there was Empirin IV, something for the stomach, Tagamint or something like that — I'm not sure — and there was another one but I can't recall what it was."

Q.   "And how much time had elapsed from the time you jumped off the exam table and the time he was writing the prescription?"

A.   "A couple of minutes."

Q.   "And did he say anything to you as he was writing the prescription? Yes or no."

A.   "Yes."

MR. BENSON   "Approach?"

THE COURT   "You may approach."

WHEREUPON THE FOLLOWING DISCUSSION WAS HELD AT THE BENCH OUTSIDE OF THE HEARING OF THE JURY:

THE COURT   "So, Mr. Benson, am I correct that when you made the statement in opening statement that the witness accused the doctor of raping her, that was not done?"

MR. BENSON   "She accused him of having sex, of having his penis out."

THE COURT "All I've understood that she has said is that, 'I saw it,' and 'Why did you zip your zipper?' "

MR. BENSON "Uh-huh."

THE COURT "I just want to be clear that's all that's been said by her. Did she say, right there in that room at that moment, 'You raped me?' "

MR. BENSON "No."

THE COURT "Okay, you had made that statement during opening and I wanted to make sure that, in the room, she never said that to him. I just want to be clear on the record. What is it you wish to elicit?"

MR. BENSON "The statement. We're now at the point that, as the doctor was writing the prescription, he makes the statement, "I need a nurse in here. This happened to me before."

THE COURT "And, Mr. Breclaw?"

MR. BRECLAW "Your Honor, this is outside the *res gestae* of the act which was the intercourse, which is clearly — if there was an intercourse — it is clear to see she was off the table; they're entering into a conversation; he has now sat her down; he is showing her the medical books, explaining the situation to her. I would think in this specific case the *res gestae* is concluded; it's not comments made while he's over her or when she accuses him of it directly, immediately as she's on the table. Secondly, it's evidence of other acts. The jury can infer that there are other acts of a similar nature where he's been accused of this type of crime, this type of activity."

THE COURT "Overruled. You may elicit the question."

WHEREUPON THE FOLLOWING PROCEEDINGS WERE ONCE AGAIN HELD IN THE HEARING OF THE JURY:

MR. BENSON

Q.   "Ms. Tammy, as the doctor was writing out the prescription and you were looking at the book, entirely what did the doctor say?"

A.   "Well, first he was writing out the prescription, and as he was writing out the prescription, he said, 'I need nurse in here. This happened to me before.' Then he was showing me the pictures of the anatomy."

THE COURT "Ladies and gentlemen of the jury, it's my duty at this time to admonish you about something. You must always keep in mind throughout the proceedings that the only issue in this case for you to resolve is whether or not the defendant had sexual intercourse with this witness when she was not aware that it was occurring. Whether or not anything else may have ever taken place on another occasion — and I refer to the incident on March 14 or an incident that may have occurred at any other time with her or any other person — does not have any bearing on whether the State has proven or not proven its case. You are not to consider what you have just heard from this witness as evidence of any other wrongdoing. It has been permitted in for the purpose to show what the doctor's reaction was to the conversation that he was having with this witness. Do you all understand that? Mr. Benson."

MR. BENSON

Q.   "After the doctor made this comment, what did you do?"

A."   "I was just sitting there. He was showing me the pictures of the female anatomy and I assume he was explaining what kind of infection I had or where it was. By then, I wasn't — I just wanted out of there. At that time, I wasn't paying attention to what he was saying."

Q.   "And did you leave?"

A.   "Yes."

Q.   "Was anyone in the reception area when you left?"

A.   "The receptionist was."

Q.   "And what, if anything, did you say or do?"

A.   "Well, I went to grab my coat. It was on the coat rack in the waiting room and I was crying, and she asked me what was wrong and I told her. I said, 'Doctor Koo just molested me,' and I told her that, 'I saw him. I felt him pushing back and forth, back and forth,' and I told her that, 'I saw it.' And I'm not really sure if she said anything to me. I know she stared at me like she didn't believe me, and I just — I just raised my hands in the air and I said, 'I swear to God,' and I left."

Q.   "And where did you go?"

A.   "To my dad's car. It was in the parking lot outside the building."

Q.   "And what happened when you got to your dad's car?"

A.   "I wasn't sure what to do. Normally, you would report this to the police, but I just — I wasn't sure what to do when it's your doctor. So I went to the pharmacy to get the prescription filled. I know the pharmacist there pretty well; she talks to me; she's real nice. I was kind of embarrassed to talk to my parents so I was going to ask her what she would do if it happened to her."

* * *

Tammy spent about 10 minutes at Walgreen's. She told the pharmacist that Dr. Koo had raped her, and she asked what the pharmacist would do if it had happened to her. In response Tammy was given three options: call the police; call the hospital's board of directors; or call the hospital's board of ethics.

Continuing her testimony, Tammy related going home and telling her mother, her father, and her sister, Becky, what had happened. Becky then called her doctor, a Munster based gynecologist, for advice and was told Tammy should call the Munster Community Hospital Board of Ethics.

Tammy called and was told by the woman who answered that she would check and get back to Tammy. (Tammy had accused Dr. Koo of rape, and Dr. Koo was on the staff of Munster Community Hospital.)

An hour later the hospital called back to tell Tammy to call the police. She did so and was told by the Hammond police that an officer would be sent out to her house and she was not to wash or change her underwear. When the officer arrived he took her statement and told her to go to St. Margaret's Hospital (in Hammond) to have a sexual assault (rape kit) test done.

She described to the jury the test details, saying, "They did the rape kit, which is a pelvic exam using the speculum. They put it inside me, and it opens up once it's inside you and then they take like a specimen. It was just like other pelvic exams. The speculum was metal; it was hard; and it was cold. Then they pulled hairs out of my head and they combed my — this is degrading; I mean what I went through was degrading — they combed my pubic areas to see if there was any — I'm not sure what for. So they combed my pubic areas and they also pulled some of my pubic hair from my pubic area.

"They took blood from me and they did a urinalysis. They took my underpants and kept them. I'm pretty sure the policeman who came to the house told me to take an extra pair because he said I wouldn't be getting them back."

"They gave me a prescription for some kind of antibiotic; they said they always do that in rape cases."

After the afternoon break Tammy resumed her testimony, telling of seeing a woman at the hospital who had come over from Haven House, a local shelter for battered women. She talked with Tammy for about 10 minutes, suggesting that Tammy schedule an appointment for rape counseling. Tammy complied and continued with the counseling program for about six months.

On the afternoon of April 3 Tammy gave two statements to the Hammond Police Department. The first was handwritten in her own words while she was alone in one of the rooms at police head-quarters. The second was in response to questions and was typed by one of the police officers.

In concluding his direct examination of Tammy, Mr. Benson asked her to compare the feeling she experienced during normal sexual relations with the feeling she experienced with Dr. Koo on March 30. She indicated the feelings were identical.

She further stated that she was not taking any drugs during the time of the trial, nor had she taken any drugs, as prescribed by Dr. Koo, since March 30, 1989.

3
Witness at Bay

July 14 • Tuesday • 3 p.m.

Defense Attorney Breclaw began his cross-examination of Tammy by addressing the defense's contention that Dr. Koo was a trusted, competent family physician. He asked questions about the statements and the deposition Tammy had made prior to the trial — two statements to the police on April 3, 1989, and one deposition on December 21, 1991.

When he attempted to have her first statement marked as an exhibit, Judge Page instructed the jury, "Prior to the trial it is not only common but almost certain that numerous statements have been taken, depositions have been taken, questions have been asked of potential witnesses so that the police that are investigating it to present the case to the prosecutor and the lawyers that are preparing for trial might know what to expect a witness to say when they take the stand. But that's the only purpose of those documents.

"Now, there is a time that the documents can be used during a trial. It can be used during the trial if one of the parties believes that a witness had said something in the courtroom during the trial that is different from something that they've said on a prior occasion, either in a statement to the police or in the deposition. They can use those statements or depositions to test the witness's memory and to see if the witness is either mistaken today or was mistaken previously, but that doesn't mean that those previous statements or those previous depositions are evidence here. We're not here to try this witness or any other witness on what may have been said at another time. You're here to judge what she or other witnesses say in front of you.''

The judge did not allow the documents to be marked as exhibits and, after a few more questions about them, Mr. Breclaw switched to questions about the testimony that Tammy had just given under direct examination by State Attorney Benson.

He questioned Tammy's conversation with her mother following the March 14 examination when Tammy thought the doctor had done something improper with his fingers in her vagina.

He highlighted her mother's advice that Tammy should trust the doctor, Tammy's concern about getting her breast x-rayed, and her general mental state of apprehension.

Then followed questions about Tammy's past medical treatment and Mr. Benson objected on the grounds of relevancy. Judge Page addressed the defense attorney directly, saying, "Mr. Breclaw, it's uncontroverted in evidence that Doctor Koo was this witness's trusted physician for 11 years prior to the alleged incident, and it would appear to be irrelevant to go into the minutiae of previous medical treatment."

Mr. Breclaw countered with, "There has been an issue raised that he doesn't refer her to specialists, and I wanted to get into that just briefly."

The judge suggested more direct questioning and the cross-exam continued with Mr. Breclaw asking another 22 questions along the same line — Tammy's medical treatment history and the fact that other doctors had become involved with her various treatments. When Mr. Benson again objected Judge Page responded with, "Previous testimony involved a referral regarding a specific complaint of the cramping and the vaginal bleeding and the abdominal pain and not regarding facial injuries in a car accident 10 or 12 years ago."

Mr. Breclaw suggested that if Dr. Koo referred her out for that, he would also refer her out for his total medical practice and care for his patients.

The Judge observed that the only issue was whether or not there was a referral out on the specific complaint in 1989. Not feeling it necessary to review the entire 11-year history of a woman with a number of problems, he sustained the objection.

The defense attorney hardly slowed down, let alone changed direction. Rather than set up a cause for appeal on grounds of not allowing defense counsel enough latitude in his cross-examination of the plaintiff, Judge Page sat back and listened to another set of questions concerning Tammy's treatment — 10 in all before Mr. Breclaw left that area.

It took another 22 questions to demonstrate that Dr. Koo had, prior to 1989, treated Tammy properly — never touched her in a sexual manner, never offered verbal sexual advances or comments, and didn't tell her any off-color jokes.

A further 30 questions surfaced the obvious — Dr. Koo spoke with a Korean accent and cadence. At first he was difficult to understand if he spoke rapidly. If he spoke slowly there was no problem.

Breclaw now addressed "the doors." He spent quite a bit of time on this subject — with Tammy and, later, with several other witnesses. He placed such emphasis on "the doors" that those two words would, for some time, conjure up a lengthy and complex scenario in the minds of anyone present in the courtroom for the entire trial.

He wanted to make a point, and Tammy's solid testimony got in his way. He felt he needed to establish in the minds of the jurors that the alleged rape took place in examination room number one, adjacent to the receptionist's office. If he could do this he could then make the point that Dr. Koo would never have engaged in sexual intercourse in a situation where someone such as his receptionist might have walked in and caught him in the act.

Tammy had testified that she was in room number two on March 30 and that she saw the doctor enter the room through a sliding door. She never wavered from that testimony.

Mr. Breclaw showed, with diagrams and recent photographs, that the hallway entrances to both exam rooms were through swinging doors. The only sliding door present in the building was between the reception office and exam room number one. That, of course, was the situation in 1992.

Tammy was pressed again and again on this subject. She was grilled about all the office details in an effort to discredit her testimony about a sliding door from the hallway to room two.

At one point she blurted out, to Mr. Breclaw's dismay, "The doors (to both exam rooms from the hallway) were sliding. I was told that they were changed later."

The defense attorney had pressed too hard and Tammy's answer had been heard by the jury. Judge Page was obligated to respond, "I should make it clear that the witness's statement that the doors had been changed is not evidence; that is classic hearsay. She didn't change the doors; she couldn't say."

Altogether, "the doors" consumed 66 questions — many of them repetitions of previous ones. The subject was covered over and over in a fruitless effort to break Tammy's basic testimony that she was in room two on March 30, 1989, and room two had a sliding door on that date. She was showing obvious strain.

Her discomfort became greater and greater as she struggled to maintain her composure. Mr. Breclaw began shifting his line of questioning toward the more intimate areas — areas that Tammy found difficult to answer when gently questioned by Mr. Benson. At times the defense attorney's abrasive and intimidating manner bothered Tammy to such an extent that many in the courtroom suffered along with her.

Under such questioning she described the interior of the examination rooms and tables. While she offered some information, the jury was never given the information they really needed — exact height of the table, exact height of the step that pulled out from its end. The table in question was not available and the jury had to make do with verbal descriptions.

Mr. Breclaw then covered the "undress below the waist, wrap the paper drape around the waist, sit on the table, scoot to the end, feet in the stirrups, taping of the paper drape to the lamp" area. He had Tammy go over this several times — attempting to show that such a sequence was normal for the well over 50 pelvic examinations Dr. Koo had given her.

In the last few questions of her first day she was asked to inform the jury that it was not Dr. Koo's practice to have a third party in the room during a pelvic examination unless so requested by the patient. Since Tammy had never thought to make such a request, most of her pelvic examinations were made without a third party present.

The judge recessed the court for the day — 63 questions after "the doors." A shaken Tammy stumbled out of the courtroom, just barely holding herself together.

Whether by accident or by design, Mr. Breclaw's questions seemed to be asked in such a manner as to degrade, discredit, and embarrass this woman. How many women could willingly subject themselves to such an ordeal? How many women would? Could this woman even consider coming back the next day for more of the same — perhaps even worse? Still, there was an aura about her and I looked forward to Wednesday morning. I was certain she'd be there.

When the bailiff led us into court that morning, the first thing we saw was Tammy in the witness box. It no longer mattered what she wore. It no longer mattered what she looked like. It was enough that she was there.

Judge Page put the jury through the "didn't see any articles or discuss the case" oath and then turned the witness over to Mr. Breclaw.

We could see Tammy brace herself for the renewal of cross-examination. Before the day was over she would be asked 1,079 questions and be instructed to return to the witness stand on Thursday morning for more.

The defense attorney began by asking her about the lamp and how it was positioned during the pelvic examination. He asked her to describe how the paper drape was taped to the lamp. The jury learned that the drape was taped by one corner to the horizontal portion of the flexible lamp so as to hang lengthwise downward and to be gathered in its center. Even so gathered it was wide enough to prevent Tammy from seeing the doctor when he moved to the end of the table. It was, however, never quite clear whether her legs (with her feet in the stirrups) ever touched the drape.

By the end of the questioning, there was very little that was clear to the jury about the exact position of the lamp in relation to the table, the doctor, or Tammy. The actual lamp and table were never produced in court. The rules of evidence did not allow substitutions because there was no way of knowing if such substitutions were accurate representations.

The line of questioning then shifted to Dr. Koo's customary practice when conducting pelvic exams. It would be difficult for anyone to remember the details of so many pelvic exams and Tammy was not always certain if a specific position or a stated sequence was always the same, mostly the same, generally the same, or seldom the same. Not that Mr. Breclaw didn't try to get the responses he wanted. He asked, over and over, if such and such was always a certain way, mostly a certain way, etc.

The judge asked Breclaw to avoid reference to these earlier 50 exams and to concentrate on the exams of March 14 and 30. The defense attorney declined the judge's request. While he explained he was trying to establish the doctor's customary practice, it seemed otherwise. Mr. Breclaw put Tammy through her entire direct testimony of the previous day three different times — the first dealing with customary practice, the second with the exam on March 14 and the third on March 30. Such an ordeal seemed to border on the obscene. No wonder, I thought, it was so difficult to get rape victims to testify.

The gloves came next. Mr. Breclaw wanted to establish that what Tammy saw as Dr. Koo's penis withdrawing from her might well have been his two fingers (as used in the bimanual portion of a pelvic exam) enclosed in surgical gloves.

To make his point he showed Tammy a pair of "tan" gloves and asked if they were like the gloves the doctor usually used. Tammy said they were much darker than those the doctor used. She testified that his usual gloves were "cream" colored, almost white, and certainly much lighter than what Breclaw was displaying to her and to the jury. The "tan" gloves were, for all intents and purposes, flesh colored.

He took a long time, but was never able to shake Tammy from her recollection that the only gloves she had ever seen Dr. Koo wear were cream colored — essentially white.

Next the defense attorney produced a disposable speculum in order to get Tammy to admit having been examined by other doctors using this plastic device, and have her testify that it did not feel cold and hard as did the steel speculum. He got as far as getting Tammy to state she had been so examined before Mr. Benson objected and the following dialogue took place.

* * *

THE COURT   "Mr. Benson's objection, as I understand it, is that there is no evidence having anything to do with a plastic speculum."

MR. BRECLAW   "Only in the sense that the plastic speculum is not cold like steel."

THE COURT   "Well, that's interesting. But how is it relevant?"

MR. BRECLAW   "Well, because on one date, she said something was inserted in her which wasn't cold like it's always been cold."

THE COURT   "Well, yes. So?"

MR. BRECLAW   "So what I'm proposing is possibly a disposable speculum was inserted in her on that day."

THE COURT   "We don't deal with possibilities here; we deal with facts. Mr. Benson has objected, and his objection would appear to be well taken."

* * *

The following questions depict the nature of Tammy's ordeal.

* * *

Q.   "During the course of a pelvic examination, was there ever a situation where Dr. Koo would put his right hand into your vagina, deep into your vagina, and move it about and move it in and out while his left hand was placed on your abdomen area?"

A.   "Yes."

Q.   "Now, when you were in for a pelvic examination, did Doctor Koo always do that?"

A.   "No, not always."

Q.   "Well, was it his normal practice during these examinations with you to sometimes just do a bimanual examination, meaning he places his hand in your vagina, feeling for organs, and not do a speculum examination?"

A. "Yes."

Q. "Now, with respect to the speculum examination, this examination was done mainly for the taking of a Pap smear, was it not?"

A. "Yes."

Q. "During part of some of the examinations, would the doctor ever feel around the lips of your vagina?"

A. "Only on March 14."

Q. "That was the only occasion that he felt around the lips of your vagina?"

A. "To the best of my knowledge, yes."

Q. "That means there's a possibility that there were other times during the examination that he felt around the lips of your vagina?"

A. "No. Other than on March 14, I don't recall."

Q. "You also indicated that when you went into the room you saw K-Y jelly on a tray?"

A. "Yes, sir."

Q. "Are you familiar with K-Y jelly?"

A. "Yes. It's a lubricant."

Q. "Now, Doctor Koo, did he not, as was part of his normal practice, did he not apply a lubricant to you prior to any pelvic examination?"

A. "When I was laying down I couldn't see; so it was there, but I'm not sure he used it."

Q. "You've been to him before and you've gone through this procedure. Did you ever feel him applying the jelly to your vagina and around the lips of your vagina?"

A.   "Not that I recall. I thought it was put on the speculum."

Q.   "You never saw it put on the speculum?"

A."   "I can't see what he's doing. I always assumed it was put on the speculum."

Q.   "And you never felt it put inside of you or on the lips of your vagina?"

A.   "No, sir."

Q.   "And you assumed it was put on the speculum?"

A."   "I just figured that, yes."

* * *

The area of "shots given by Dr. Koo for pain" was covered at great length. Tammy stuck to her previous testimony that all shots for pain were after her exams except on March 30 when she received the shot prior to the exam. She also repeated that the shot on March 30 was in the arm — in contrast to all the others being in the buttocks area.

Mr. Breclaw now zeroed in on March 14 and Tammy once again confirmed her visit as due to a white fluid discharge, pain, bloating, and vaginal bleeding. He started the K-Y jelly questioning again and Tammy began to loose her composure. Judge Page suggested it was time for the midmorning break. After the break, Mr. Breclaw continued as follows.

* * *

Q.   "And would your feet be in the stirrups?"

A.   "Yes."

Q.   "And your knees would be pointing straight up into the air?"

A.   "They're like out."

Q.   "Out. Okay, that's pointing up?"

A.   "Yes."

Q.   "Then he takes the paper cloth and drapes it on an over-head light of some type?"

A.   "Yes."

Q.   "And this was a normal procedure, correct?"

A.   "With me, yes."

Q.   "Did he, if you can recall, take the jelly and use it to lu-bricate your vaginal area?"

A."   "I don't recall."

Q.   "Did he place a speculum inside of your vagina?"

A.   "Yes."

Q.   "With respect to the speculum, I think you testified it felt cold?"

A.   "Yes. Cold, hard; it was steel."

Q.   "You don't remember if he lubricated the area, the vagi-nal area prior to inserting the speculum?"

A.   "I don't think so. I always thought that he lubricated the speculum."

Q.   "Now, he inserts the speculum, correct?"

A.   "Yes, sir."

Q.   "And did he then take a Q-tip and take any samples in-side of your vaginal area for a Pap smear.?"

A.   "I don't recall. I can't see."

Q.   "Well, did you feel anything going into your vagina, any type of gauze or any type of instrument other than the speculum?"

A.   "Yes, but I couldn't see so I'm not sure what it was."

Q.   "You're not sure what it was. So while the speculum was in you, you felt something going inside and you're not sure what it was because you couldn't see it?"

A.   "Yes."

Q.   "But you felt this sensation before on prior examinations while the speculum was inside of you?"

A.   "On the fourteenth, yes."

Q.   "Even though you said you didn't know, is it in your mind probable that he was taking a Pap smear?"

A.   "Yes."

Q.   "There comes a time when you stated you felt fingers around the lips of your vagina?"

A.   "Yes."

Q.   "Is this while the speculum is still inserted in your vagina or while the speculum is out of your vagina, or if you know? "

A.   "Both. I felt it on my vagina while the speculum was inside me and the speculum was taken out and then his fingers were still there — I still felt the fingers there."

Q.   "With respect to the bimanual movement, something you had never felt before, you testified to, were these unusual movements in your vaginal area, were they while the speculum was in your vagina?"

A.   "Yes."

Q.   "And what were the sensations that you felt?"

A.   "Going back and forth on the lips of my vagina."

Q.   "Was the speculum also moving in your vagina?"

A.   "I don't recall. I don't think it was."

Q.   "At this time, by the way, when you were in his office, did you take codeine, aspirin with codeine, or a codeine product that day for pain?"

A.   "I don't recall."

Q.   "Did you take Valium that day, the fourteenth?"

A.   "No."

Q. "You don't recall if you took codeine or not but you can recall that you didn't take Valium?"

A. "I usually took the Valium at night to go to sleep. I never took it during the day."

Q. "Did you take Valium the night before the fourteenth?"

A." "Probably, yes." ·

Q. "You had been taking codeine on a regular basis, correct?"

A. "Yes, when I had pain, I would take it."

Q. "And were you in pain that day?"

A. "Yes."

Q. "Most probably you were taking codeine that day for pain?"

A. "Yes, probably."

Q. "Now, you're not seeing all of this, you're just feeling this, right?"

A. "Yes."

Q. "You testified you didn't know what was touching your vagina, is that what you're saying? Or are you saying it was his fingers?"

A. "I believe it was. I didn't see them, but it wasn't the speculum and it didn't feel like a Q-tip."

Q. "So Mr. Benson mentioned to you that it might have been a tongue. You would know the difference, would you not?"

A. "I said when he asked me yesterday, I said I believe that would be wet; there would be a difference in a tongue and a finger, yes."

Q. "There would be a difference?"

A. "I believe so, yes; yes, definitely."

Q.   "You never told him it was a tongue?"

A.   "No, sir."

Q.   "In your opinion, it was always a finger that was touching the lips of your vagina?"

A.   "On March 14, yes."

Q.   "And not some other part of his anatomy, for example, it was not his penis?"

A.   "Yes, sir. I believe it was his fingers."

Q.   "After he took the speculum from your vagina, what did he do next?"

A.   "His fingers were there for a few seconds and that was about it."

Q.   "What do you mean that was about it?"

A.   "That was about it. His fingers were still there moving for a few seconds and the speculum was already out."

Q.   "What was the moving type of action?"

A.   "Back and forth on the lips of my vagina."

Q.   "Would you show me with your hands what you mean by back and forth?"

A.   "Like that [indicating], back and forth, to the left and to the right."

Q.   "It was not in and out?"

A.   "He moved them on the inside of me too, after the speculum was pulled out."

Q.   "I asked you what the movements were of the fingers and you said they were around the circumference of the vagina."

A.   "You said on the lips of the vagina, sir. He also inserted them in my vagina; there's a difference."

Q. "Then there was a bimanual examination that we talked about where he put his hand into your vagina and he put his other hand on top of your stomach, did he not?"

A. "No."

Q. "He never did that on that day?"

A. "On that day he did earlier, but not when his fingers were moving around, no."

Q. "On March 14 did Doctor Koo place his fingers deep inside of your vagina and move them around?"

A. "Yes, before. Yes, I believe it was before he put the speculum in, he just like pressed on my stomach to feel where the pain was, and he had his fingers up in, and then he used the speculum."

Q. "First of all March 14, did he, in fact, stick his fingers in your vagina with his hand on top of your stomach?"

A. "Yes, sir."

Q. "Was that done after or before he did the speculum?"

A. "It was before the speculum."

Q. "Now, was it is customary practice in the other examinations when there was both the speculum examination and the exam with his fingers deep into your vagina, was it his customary practice to do that before he did the speculum examination."

A. "Yes."

Q. "So you're saying he would first do an examination of placing his fingers deep into your vagina and then do a speculum examination?"

A. "Sometimes he just pressed on my stomach to see where it hurt, but other times he would press on my stomach and have his fingers in. I don't know what he's doing — organs or something, or sometimes he's just pressing on my stomach. Other times, his hand is there with the pressing on my stomach.''

Q.   "On March 14 he used a speculum and probably took a Pap smear. He also did a deep intrusion into your vagina with his right fingers and his left hand on top of your stomach?''

A.   "Yes."

Q.   "And he was also touching the lips of your vagina?"

A.   "This was like — this was after — when his hands were pressing on my stomach and he had his fingers up inside me with his hand pressing on my stomach, that was before the speculum was put in me. Then the speculum was put in me and that's when he was moving his fingers around the lips of my vagina."

Q.   "Where his fingers are on the outside of your vagina, you indicated that they were in a circular type of movement, correct?"

A.   "I said back and forth. It was like that [indicating], like to the left and the right."

Q.   "So this had never been done to you before, correct?"

A.   "Correct."

Q.   "In your deposition of December 4, 1991, did you ever characterize this as foreplay?"

A.   "Yes, sir."

Q.   "Is that what you felt on March 14, 1989, that Doctor Koo was engaging in foreplay with you?"

A.   "That's what it felt like, yes."

Q.   "And that's what you thought?"

A.   "Yes, sir."

Q.   "On March 14, 1989?"

A.   "Yes, sir.

Q.   "Do you recall making a statement to the police on April 3 where you stated, 'Then he used his fingers inside me moving them around and for too long a time, but for what, I still don't know?' "

A.   "Yes, sir.

Q.   "So it would be accurate, would it not, that on March 14, you did not know how to characterize what his actions were?"

MR. BENSON   "Object. That's argumentative."

MR. BRECLAW   "I'm trying to get an answer to —"

MR. BENSON   "I would object. That's misquoting the witness. She said, 'It felt like foreplay,' not that it was, but it felt like it."

MR. BRECLAW   "Well, the jury heard the evidence."

THE COURT   "Yes, the jury heard the evidence, so I'll not comment on what I thought I heard or what you two thought you heard. It's for the jury to recall her response."

MR. BRECLAW

Q.   "Did you not state that on March 14, to this jury, that you felt that Doctor Koo was engaging in foreplay with you?"

A."   "I believe I said it felt like foreplay."

Q.   "In your mind, did you believe that he was engaging in foreplay?"

A.   "That's what it felt like."

Q.   "And that was what was in your mind?"

A.   "That's what it felt like, yes."

Q.   "And that was a concern you had?"

A.   "Yes."

Q.   "But nowhere in this statement did you say that you felt Doctor Koo was engaging in foreplay with you?"

A.   "I wasn't sure if I could use those words."

Q.   "What you did say was, 'He used his fingers inside me moving them around and for too long a time, but for what, I still don't know.' You made that statement?"

A.   "Yes."

Q.   "Now, how much time were these fingers moving around in that type of motion?"

A.   "A couple of minutes."

Q.   "Why is that "too long a time"?"

A.   "In my opinion, it shouldn't have taken that long if it was something medical."

Q.   "So this is within your mind when you say it just took too long of a time if it was something medical?"

A.   "Yes. I couldn't understand why it was happening that long."

Q.   "Because in your mind, you characterized this action as foreplay?"

A.   "Yes, sir."

Q.   "And that it was not a medical procedure?"

A.   "I don't believe so, no."

Q.   "At the time, did you make any complaint to the doctor, say, 'Doctor, what are you doing to me?' "

A.   "No."

Q.   "Did you ask the doctor what he did to you?"

A.   "No."

Q.   "Did you state to any member of his staff or make a complaint to them of what he was doing to you?"

A.   "No."

Q.   "You made no complaint at all?"

A.   "No, sir."

Q.   "Asked no questions at all?"

A.   "No, sir."

Q.   "Now, was the doctor, when he was doing this finger motion on your vagina, was the doctor breathing hard?"

A.   "I don't believe — I can't recall. I couldn't see him. If he was, I didn't hear it."

Q.   "Do you remember during your deposition being asked the question on page 132, 'Okay, was he breathing hard at that time? Did you hear any hard breathing?' Do you remember being asked that question?"

A.   "I can't recall all the depositions. I don't remember that part."

Q.   "Do you remember answering no to that question?"

A.   "I just now said no, so I believe so — that's correct."

Q.   "Let's start over. On March 14 — as he had his fingers on your vagina, going back and forth on your vagina, was the doctor breathing hard?"

A.   "I don't think so, no. I didn't hear it and I couldn't see him. I don't think so."

Q.   "You didn't hear any breathing?"

A.   "No, sir."

Q.   "Did the doctor make any comment to you?"

A.   "No, sir."

Q.   "And you heard nothing from him?"

A.   "No."

Q.   "To make it perfectly clear, at this time in your mind, you characterize this action as foreplay?"

A.   "At the time, I wasn't sure, but now, yes."

Q.   "Well, in your mind on March 14, you stated several times that the actions felt like foreplay and that it was in your mind foreplay."

A.   "I'm not sure I understand the question, because at the time I didn't think he would do something like that. Then after what actually happened on March 30, that's what I believe it to be. My statement was taken after March 30."

Q.   "So what you're saying now is on March 14, you did not believe his actions were foreplay?"

A.   "I suspected it, but I thought there had to be some medical term for it because I didn't — I trusted him."

Q.   "Well, you suspected on March 14 in his office that he was engaging in foreplay with you. Is that your testimony?"

A.   "Yes, sir, that's what I believe now."

Q.   "Well, on the fourteenth?"

A.   "I wasn't sure. I thought there had to be some kind of medical term — medical thing for it because I didn't think he'd do something like that."

Q.   "On March 14, going back to March 14, did you suspect that he might be engaging in foreplay with you in his office?"

A.   "I'm not sure; I wasn't sure. I suspected but I didn't think he would do something like that."

Q.   "It was only until after March 30 that you then now are totally sure that March 14, he was engaging in foreplay with you?"

A.   "That's what I believe, yes."

Q.   "And now there's no doubt in your mind today that he was engaging in foreplay with you on March 14, 1989."

A.   "That's what it felt like."

MR. BENSON   "Objection. Relevancy, Your Honor."

THE COURT   "Relevancy?"

MR. BENSON   "The question has been asked and answered at least seven or eight times what she thinks today."

THE COURT   "I understand Mr. Breclaw to be getting ready to move on to a new area."

* * *

The strain was now so familiar to Tammy that she was able to handle Breclaw's questions with little show of emotion and less change of expression. While generally facing the jury, her eyes went far beyond the courtroom. It was her voice that became the mirror of her inner thoughts. There was anger and fear. But so was there resolve, defiance, and disdain.

Buffeted by the defense attorney's relentless series of intimate questions, Tammy somehow managed to retain her composure through most of her testimony. She was incapable of theatrics. There was no weeping for effect. When she had trouble with her emotions so did everyone in the courtroom. She had told her story so many times to so many detectives and attorneys that her testimony before the jury was clear and consistent. She was long past the point of embarrassment — or so it seemed. As question after question exposed her most personal thoughts and feelings, it became impossible for anyone in the courtroom not to suffer with her.

Breclaw's next question was about what Tammy had told her mother and the tension in the courtroom vanished as the defense did move to a new area.

The relief was brief, however, as it became obvious that this new area contained the same old subject. Tammy was asked about what she told her mother concerning the doctor's use of his fingers on March 14. And there we were — listening to Tammy go through it all over again.

How did she describe the doctor's activities to her mother? Did she convey her feelings of foreplay to her mother? What words did she use? How did her mother react? What did she say? Did she understand the sexual implication of Tammy's story?

Mr. Breclaw then put Tammy through her visit to the doctor on March 28. He reviewed the doctor's list of her problems — yeast infection, fallopian tube infection, cyst on her ovaries. Finally he reached March 30 and asked Tammy to repeat what she was wearing for her afternoon visit to the doctor's office — tennis shoes, gray sweat pants, T-shirt, underpants and bra. She had not put on any makeup or done anything with her hair. She had pain along with her other symptoms.

She testified that she was taking the codeine Dr. Koo had prescribed but had not taken any Valium on the evening of March 29. She said she didn't always take the Valium — just when she needed it to get to sleep.

July 15 • Wednesday • noon

Judge Page adjourned the court for lunch, and I took a mental journey to the land of repetition.

Attorneys use repetition to emphasize a point; to stall while they work out their next line of questioning; to develop different perspectives; to check the statement of one witness with that of another; to test the credibility of a witness. But most of all, they use it to break a witness. A strong witness prevails; a weak witness does not.

4
Endurance

July 15 • Wednesday • 1:15 p.m.

In an attempt to confuse the witness, Mr. Breclaw abruptly changed the time line of his questions. Beginning with the events of March 30, 1989, he went to the point when Tammy was leaving the doctor's office after the alleged rape and worked his way back in time. He would then reverse direction, begin at a point in time before the main event, and work his way forward to when she felt penetrated by something warm.

He began by asking Tammy what the doctor did to her just before she left the examining room on March 30.

She indicated receiving a prescription and noted that she was very upset and crying. Asked what happened before Dr. Koo gave her the prescription she mentioned the anatomy book with the pictures of the female anatomy, the comments about needing a nurse in the exam room, the doctor guiding her to the chair, and finally her comments about his zipper.

With each incident Mr. Breclaw questioned her on her mental state. Was she upset? Was she crying? Was she very upset? Was she highly upset? Was she highly upset and crying? Was she in a state of shock?

When he didn't get the answer he wanted he would repeat the question over and over. At one point, in response to one of the many objections from Mr. Benson, Judge Page told the defense attorney, "I'm not challenging your right to cross-examine. I just don't want the area repeated over and over and over. There has been a little bit of that."

By then many of the jurors were taking notes and the judge felt it necessary to caution us as follows. "If you want to take notes," he said, "and I notice that some of you are, it is difficult to take detailed notes and pay attention to what the witnesses are saying at the same time. If you do take notes, be sure that the taking of notes does not interfere with your listening to and considering all the evidence. Also, if you do take notes, do not discuss them with anyone before you have begun your deliberations. Do not take notes with you at the end of the day. If you are taking notes, I will ask you to turn them over to the bailiff so that they may be safely kept. I would remind you again it is your right to take notes, especially considering the length that this trial is expected to be, but be sure to leave them with the bailiffs at the end of the day. If you chose not to take notes, remember it is your responsibility to listen carefully to the evidence. You cannot give this responsibility to someone who is taking notes. We depend on the judgment of all members of the jury; you must all remember the evidence in the case.

"You will notice that we do have an official court reporter making a record of the trial (audio tape and shorthand). However, we will not have typewritten transcripts of this record available for use in reaching your decision in this case. If during deliberations you find that there is a serious disagreement among you as to what was or was not said, it is possible to have the testimony of a witness replayed, but you must keep in mind that if you ask for a witness's testimony to be replayed, all of it from beginning to end, direct, cross, redirect, and recross must all be played.

"Nothing that I say should discourage you from taking notes. It is my job, however, to make sure you're aware of those limitations."

The intensity of Mr. Breclaw's cross-examination began to grow as he approached the critical area. A hushed courtroom hung on every word.

* * *

MR. BRECLAW

Q. "Just prior to pulling out the book on the female anatomy, what did you say to him?"

TAMMY:

A. "I told him, 'I saw it.' "

Q. "You told him you saw it, is that what you said?"

A. "Yes, yes."

Q. "And what did he say to you?"

A. "He said, "No." And I said, "I saw you zip your zipper," and he motioned down and he said they were zipped. I said, "Well, I just saw you zip them."

Q. "Just prior to the book — the book, now — did you tell him you saw it, or did you tell him, 'I saw you zip your zipper.' "?

A. " 'I saw you zip your zipper,' " that was prior, yes."

Q. "And what did he say?"

A. "He said, 'They're zipped.' "

Q. "Did he have a facial expression?"

A. "No."

Q. "You asked him did he zip his zipper? Is that what you said to him?"

A.   "No, I said, 'I saw you zip your zipper.' I asked him, 'Why did you zip your zipper?' He motioned, he said, 'They're zipped,' and I said, 'Yeah, I just saw you zip them.' "

Q.   "Now, were you practically hysterical at that time?"

A.   "I don't think I was hysterical. I was very emotional at the time."

Q.   Do you remember on page 2 of the typewritten statement, "He looked down at his pants and motioned with his hands by his pants and said, 'They're zipped.' I told him I saw him zip them up and I was practically hysterical by then and I just wanted to get dressed." Practically hysterical, would that be an accurate representation of your mental state at that point?"

A.   "I said practically, yes."

Q.   "Now, you did not hear him zip his zipper, did you?"

A.   "Yes, I did; I heard the zipper."

Q.   "You heard the zipper?"

A.   "Yes, sir."

Q.   "Now, you did not testify to that on direct examination. You're aware of that?"

A.   "Yes. I'm aware of what you just said."

Q.   "You stated that you saw Doctor Koo's penis during the direct examination."

A.   "Yes."

Q.   "Did this penis have a condom on it?"

A.   "I don't think so. I can't remember that. It was too quick — it was a second — but I know what I saw."

Q.   "Well, you don't know if he had — "

A.   "Honestly, no."

Q.   "Was the penis that you saw, did that have the same color of skin as Doctor Koo?"

A.   "It was too quick to tell. It was one second."

Q.   "Or was it a fraction of a second?"

A.   "Maybe."

Q.   "Was your answer maybe?"

A.   "It was just quick. Maybe; I'm not sure."

Q.   "A glimpse?"

A.   "A quick glimpse, yes. Just like as it pulled out."

Q.   "A fleeting glimpse?"

A.   "Yes, but it was attached to his body."

Q.   "It was attached to his body?"

A.   "Yes."

Q.   "Was his penis circumcised?"

A.   "I don't know; I didn't see it for that long."

Q.   "Did you see the tip of the front part of the penis where it ended."

A.   "No, it was too quick."

Q.   "You saw part of this penis?"

A.   "All I know is what I saw; it was attached to his body. I couldn't tell how long or anything; it was too quick to tell."

Q.   "You didn't see his zipper open?"

A.   "I didn't really notice that part. I was just shocked at what I saw."

Q.   "And at the time you saw this, it was being pulled out of you?"

A.   "Yes, sir."

Q.   "And this was at a time that you were on your back look-
       ing under a sheet that was draped, correct?"

A.   "Yes, sir."

Q.   "Couldn't that have been Doctor Koo in this fashion [in-
       dicating]?"

A.   "No, sir."

Q.   "Pardon?"

A.   "No, sir. His hands were on my body. No, sir, unless he
       has a third hand?"

Q.   "So you did not see his hands on your body?"

A.   "I felt them. I could see up — this part of his hands [indi-
       cating]."

MR. BENSON:

"Judge, I would object to this question. She has already testified that what Mr. Breclaw has on his hand is not the glove he was
wearing, so that's improper impeachment, Your Honor."

THE COURT:

"That would be allowable under cross-examination. However,
Mr. Breclaw, you do need to make it clear for the sake of the written record what it is you're doing at the time so that someone reading the record of this proceeding would be able to understand what
has just occurred in court. For clarification of the record, Mr. Breclaw took what appears to be a latex-type glove and put it over his
right hand and held it in front of his crotch and asked the witness
the questions that are on the record already."

* * *

What Judge Page did not read into the record was the manner in
which Mr. Breclaw performed this little act. He closed his right
hand and then extended the forefinger and index finger together so

as to give a best approximation of a penis. Holding the fingers in front of his crotch he began to approach Tammy until she recoiled in horror at what she was seeing."

* * *

MR. BRECLAW

   Q.   "Now, you stated that it couldn't have been that hand un-less he had a third hand. Was that your comment?"

TAMMY

   A.   "Yes, sir."

   Q.   "You did not see his hands on any other portion of your body?"

   A.   "Not his hands, his arms."

   Q.   "When you lifted up?"

   A.   "When I lifted up — under the paper drape."

   Q.   "Did the doctor ejaculate in you?"

   A.   "He didn't have time, no."

   Q.   "How long was he in you?"

   A.   "A minute or two. It seemed like forever, but it couldn't have been more than a couple of minutes."

   Q.   "In your opinion, that would not have been enough time for him to ejaculate?"

MR. BENSON:

   "Objection, Your Honor, that's argumentative."

THE COURT:

   "Mr. Breclaw, the operative question I believe is whether or not the witness sensed an ejaculation. Anything else would be speculation."

MR. BRECLAW:

Q. "On page 179, line 23, do you remember being asked the question, "All right, when you saw this, was it a glimpse of the entire penis or a portion of the penis?" Answer, "It was — I'm not really sure. I know it was attached to his body. I saw it for just a quick second."

A. "Yes, sir."

Q. "So on this date, does not your answer indicate that you do not know whether it was the entire penis or just a portion of the penis?"

A. "I'm not sure; it was too quick. I don't know."

Q. "Now, you saw this penis that was in his crotch area, correct?"

A. "Yes."

Q. "And you did not see his zipper open?"

THE WITNESS:

"I'm sorry. Can I take a break? [Witness crying.]"

* * *

The parenthetical comment in the record doesn't even come close to describing what was happening. For some time now, Mr. Breclaw's voice, manner, and body language displayed his disdain for Tammy. His manner was abrasive, strident, contemptuous, and aggressive. Judge Page normally sent the jury from the courtroom before anyone else. But this time it was the witness who was allowed to leave first. A full half-hour later we returned to be advised by the judge as follows.

"Ladies and gentlemen of the jury, as we broke, one of the jurors in the hall stopped me and asked about questions.

"As I indicated to you in your preliminary instructions, it is possible to have questions addressed to the witness. In order for that to occur, you must put your question in writing while that witness is still on the stand. If I determine that the question is one that the rules of law permit to be asked, then I will ask it of the witness. I would prefer not to bring your questions up until after we have had both direct and cross-examination for the reason that your question may very well yet be answered by questions that are about to be asked by the attorneys.''

As the judge was speaking I couldn't keep from glancing at the witness box to see if Tammy had regained her composure. She appeared nervous and uncomfortable as the judge continued with his instructions. Then she glanced toward the prosecutor's table as Mr. Benson made some gesture with his hand. She sat up straight and smiled — the nervousness gone.

* * *

MR. BRECLAW:

Q. "Mrs. Garza, I won't be just but two or three more questions on this particular area and I'll be away from it. Would it be true to say that the portion of whatever you saw did not have any identifying marks on it?"

A. "I couldn't tell you; it was too quick."

Q. "In fact, on December 4, you were asked a question on page 180, "Did you see the head or the tip of the penis or are we talking the root or where it starts that you saw?" Answer, "More where it starts I think.""

A. "Yes."

Q. "When you put the phrase, "More where it starts," what did you mean by that statement?"

A. "Towards the body."

Q. "So it was a brief glimpse. And what you're telling me is that I could ask a lot of dumb questions about the penis but you wouldn't be able to get me much of a description. Is that a fair statement?''

A.   Yes. I said I couldn't describe it.''

* * *

Mr. Breclaw continued his review of Tammy's previous statements, depositions, and testimony. The subject of the zipper and Dr. Koo's penis getting back inside his pants was covered by more questions than I thought possible to create about a relatively simple action.

The Q-tip cleansing and sharp object jabbing were next to be explored to the extreme. Mr. Breclaw again reversed the time frame and asked Tammy about when she was on the exam table before the incident of penetration. She said she was a bit light-headed but otherwise aware of what was going on.

He made a big thing about her not kicking the doctor in the groin when she experienced the feeling of rape. She maintained her previous position of not being sure and of not really believing the doctor would do something like that. By the time she saw the penis withdraw he was already turning away.

* * *

Q.   "Well, he goes to a cabinet and gets — he guides you gently to a chair and then he pulls out a book and starts to show you pictures of the female anatomy and tries to explain what your medical condition was, did he not?''

A.   "Yes.''

Q.   "He then fills out a prescription for you, does he not?''

A.   "Yes.''

Q.   "He then hands you the prescription?''

A.   "Yes.''

Q.　"Are not these the actions of a physician who is caring for his patient?"

A.　"He didn't care for me. He raped me. That's not caring — I'm sorry — that's not caring."

* * *

One would need to listen to the taped transcript of the trial to appreciate how Tammy's answer — loud, clear, and filled with anger — literally stunned the courtroom. Several moments passed before Mr. Breclaw recovered enough to do what he always did when he didn't get the answer he was seeking. He simply repeated the question.

Mr. Benson objected and was sustained by Judge Page. Tammy did not respond to the question a second time. She was still shaking from the force of her first response.

The cross-examination continued through the areas of what examination room (number two), did it have a sliding door (yes), and what was the effect of the shot in her right arm (light-headed, not sleepy, not drowsy). Questions concerning the doctor's lab coat (did he wear it that day; was it open or buttoned shut) were generally a waste of time — Tammy just didn't remember anything about a lab coat that day.

Under additional questioning she stated she took Valium in pill form to help her get to sleep on most, but not all, nights when she went to bed. The shot given her by Dr. Koo did not cause her to become sleepy like the Valium pills, but she felt the light-headedness almost at once — much quicker than she had ever felt the effects of the pills.

For some time now, Mr. Benson had raised objection after objection to Mr. Breclaw's questions. This often led to open conversations between the judge and the attorneys before a ruling was made.

At one point when Tammy was asked if she understood the question she answered, "You guys lost me."

Sometime later, under like conditions, she exclaimed, "You guys are losing me."

Judge Page responded to her second comment with, "We lawyers tend to do that sometimes."

A major contention of the defense was that Tammy was under the influence of Valium and codeine at the time she felt she was raped. Mr. Breclaw set out to convince the jury that her feeling was a drug induced fantasy. To do so he decided to explore the area of prescriptions — as written, as filled, as taken.

His questions then began to focus on how these prescriptions were written and how they could be refilled. He covered three pharmacies in the area but concentrated on Fairmeadows pharmacy in Munster.

Much of his evidence concerning the specific drugs and the specific quantities taken could not be presented to the court until the prosecutor had completed his presentation. However, a certain amount of testimony was needed from Tammy to lay the proper foundation for various prescription records to be later placed in evidence.

For that reason the judge allowed Mr. Breclaw to get that testimony into the record now so that Tammy would not be required to return several days later as a witness for the defense.

In addition to the details printed on a typical prescription pad concerning refill practice, the jury was made aware of a five-page computer printout containing a list of prescriptions that had been filled in Tammy's name.

Judge Page cautioned the jury about what was going on. He made sure that we all understood that there was no evidence at this time that Tammy had actually received the drugs so listed or, even if she had, that she had taken them.

What we did learn was that the quantities of codeine and Valium indicated as filled by a given pharmacy were two to three times the quantities prescribed by the doctor for the time periods involved.

While Tammy may not have actually taken all these drugs, she seemed rather casual about the quantities purchased. And that thought cracked open the pandora's box for the first time.

It appeared Tammy had been making numerous visits to the doctor and getting large quantities of drugs. And Tammy was not, by any means, in a financial position to be paying for any of this. She was unemployed, single, and the mother of a young girl. This was a welfare situation. Medicaid was picking up the entire tab, and I, along with other taxpayers, was paying for her drugs. No wonder Tammy never bothered to keep track of her pills. When she ran low all she had to do was pick up the phone, call Fairmeadows Pharmacy, and more would be delivered to her doorstep.

Mr. Breclaw's questioning raised a number of possibilities that would account for the apparent oversupply of drugs. Tammy could be taking massive quantities herself or selling them on the side. Her sister, Becky, could be doing likewise. He next had Tammy tell the jury that she had filed a civil case against Dr. Koo. That case was on hold pending the outcome of the criminal trial. In this manner the defense attorney raised questions concerning the testimony of a witness (Tammy) who stood to gain financially through civil action if Dr. Koo were found guilty in criminal court.

At this point the judge directed, with jury agreement, that the trial go beyond the 4:00 p.m. quitting time to 5:30 p.m. in the hope that Tammy's testimony could be completed that day. Mr. Breclaw's next move made such a hope an impossible dream.

* * *

THE FOLLOWING DISCUSSION WAS HELD AT THE BENCH OUTSIDE OF THE HEARING OF THE JURY:

MR. BRECLAW

"Judge, the witness has stated that she, after this occurred, didn't know who to contact, what authorities to contact because of this rape, and I'm at this time in the position to offer evidence that she has on two other occasions claimed that she has been raped and on one of the occasions, at least, that she has gone to the police. And I ask your permission to go into these matters at this time on cross- examination."

THE COURT

"Overruled. Permission is denied. The prejudicial value of that information far outweighs the probativeness."

MR. BRECLAW

"I have also, Your Honor, tendered interrogatories to the prosecutor for Ms. Garza to answer pursuant to an agreement we worked out between us, and those interrogatories have not been answered yet and I cannot continue on with my cross-examination or finish it until such time as they are. I would then request to conclude the cross-examination now subject to reopening it when the interrogatories are given back to me."

* * *

The judge dismissed the jury for the day, recessed the court until 9:45 a.m., Thursday, and told Tammy to remain in the witness box. He indicated to the court reporter that the proceedings were still to be recorded for the record. He then instructed Mr. Benson to give Mr. Breclaw the list of agreed questions for the witness to answer.

* * *

MR. BRECLAW

Q. "Would you please list any and all prior allegations of rape that you made to anyone?"

A. "I was raped when I was 18-years-old, December 24, 1979."

Q. "Have you ever told anyone that you were raped on any other occasion?"

A. "I told the Hammond Clinic that my boyfriend had — it wasn't really a rape, but he had forced me, and I just — it was willing, but they might have put it down as rape. I did not say the word rape. It was sometime in 1988, but I'm not sure exactly when."

Q. "Would you please list the alleged perpetrator of each alleged rape? First of all, the 1979 rape."

A. "I don't know."

Q. "With respect to the 1988 rape, that allegation of rape made to personnel at the Hammond Clinic?"

A. "In my mind, it wasn't rape, but the Hammond Clinic might have put it down — might have construed it as rape, but in my mind, it wasn't."

Q. "You testified that you made this allegation in 1988 to personnel at the Hammond Clinic. Now, what was the name of that person?"

MR. BENSON

"Object, Your Honor. This is the whole problem with the interrogatories. It's about her interpretation of the word rape. She indicated it was a forced sexual encounter with no threats. Now, I don't know if counsel's interrogatory means to include that as rape or not. And I know what he's getting at, but I don't know how she can possibly answer the question. I would object to this as being vague."

THE COURT

"The witness shall not be compelled to give the name; the person may be referred to by reference as you have done for the sake of your further questioning."

MR. BRECLAW

Q.   "Please state whether any police or law enforcement agency was notified of each alleged rape."

A.   "In 1979, yes, to the Hammond Police Department."

Q.   "In 1988?"

MR. BENSON

"I would object, Your Honor. She said that wasn't a rape in her mind; it was a forced sexual encounter. The question is inapplicable."

THE COURT

"Mr. Breclaw, your next interrogatory."

MR. BRECLAW

Q.   "State which allegations were not true."

A.   "None."

THE COURT

"The record should be clear that based on pretrial discussions the purpose of this questioning is to determine if this witness has ever made a previous allegation of rape which she later recanted or which can demonstrably be shown not to be true."

Q.   "Regarding the incident in 1988 with the individual that you have identified as your boyfriend, did you ever make an accusation against him of rape?"

THE WITNESS

A.   "In those exact words, no."

Q.   "As to whatever words you may have put to it, did you ever later deny that the incident in question had taken place?"

A.   "No."

THE COURT

"Mr. Breclaw, this seems to exhaust the area for which the court permitted delayed discovery."

MR. BRECLAW

"It appears to me she is denying today that she was ever raped by her boyfriend in 1988. She's denying that to us. Would you agree with that? May I ask her that question?"

THE COURT

"She has said that it was not what she would call rape, that is was a forced sexual encounter."

MR. BRECLAW

"A forced sexual encounter appears to me that it is against her consent because force was applied to her."

THE COURT

"I agree with you within the area of semantics, but she has said that she never made an accusation of it."

MR. BRECLAW

"She told the personnel at the Hammond Clinic that, "Her ex-boyfriend is a junkie and recently raped the patient. That is the reason the patient needs an Aids test."

THE COURT

> Q.   "Are you denying the sexual encounter to which Mr.
>   Breclaw refers by his questions ever took place?"

THE WITNESS

> A.   "No, I don't deny that."

MR. BRECLAW

"Well, I'm simply stating that we offer to prove to the Court
that she has made an allegation of rape against her ex-boyfriend
and now she is stating, if effect, that there wasn't a rape, it was
something other fhan a rape."

THE COURT

"Is that everything? Is there anything else?"

MR. BRECLAW

"Can I have this exhibit marked and made part of the record?"

THE COURT

"We take your word for it that that's what that document would
show, that someone else gave it the name of rape. But a rose is a
rose is a rose."

MR. BRECLAW

"I'm claiming that she told this person that she was raped."

THE COURT

"She's not denying now that the sexual encounter took place.
That's the essence of that exception. And if you read those cases
closely, you'll see that."

MR. BRECLAW

"But she's saying she wasn't raped today."

THE COURT

"That is an argument over semantics."

MR. BRECLAW

"Can I ask her straight out, "Were you raped in 1988 by your boyfriend?""

THE COURT

"Yes, go ahead."

MR. BRECLAW

Q.   "Were you raped in 1988 by your boyfriend?"

MR. BENSON

"Objection. It calls for a legal conclusion that this witness is incompetent to give."

THE COURT

"Sustained."

MR. BRECLAW

Q.   "In 1988 did your boyfriend insert his penis in your vagina against your will and without your consent?"

THE WITNESS

"Do I have to answer yes or no?"

THE COURT

"Answer in the way you best can."

THE WITNESS:

A.   "To me, it wasn't rape. I did it just to get him out of my
face. He had beaten me up before. I wanted him away
from me, so I did it to get him out of my face, just to get
rid of him. He didn't really force me; I did it just to get
him away from me."

*   *   *

Breclaw continued to argue the point in order to place
Tammy's sexual past before the jury. He was grasping at one of the
exceptions to the Indiana Rape Shield law and Judge Page countered with, "The case as I remember was a child who accused an
adult of a sexual encounter and that the child later recanted it and
said that it never happened."

He then denied Mr. Breclaw's request to question Tammy in
front of the jury, saying, "It would become merely an argument
over semantics and would, I believe, create side issues that need
not be resolved in this case. And the issue in this case is whether or
not there was any sexual meeting of the genitals of the two individuals in question, by whatever name you want to give it. As I understand it, the defense is that it never happened and she says that it
did. The name that that is to be given is for the jury to say."

July 16 • Thursday • 9:00 a.m.

The defense attorney resumed his cross-examination with the
following disclaimer: "Mrs. Garza, I'm going to go back to March
30 but want to put your mind at ease that I will not be questioning
you with respect to a description of whatever it was that you saw
pulling away from your body."

His next questions covered the exam table, the lab coat, the
lamp, and the pull-out step. The only answer the jury had not heard
before was that Tammy was five-feet, 10-inches tall.

Mr. Benson had enough. He asked to approach the bench where he said, "Judge, so far there has not been one question that has been asked this morning that was not already asked and answered yesterday, and I believe this is just an attempt by counsel to upset the witness in view of her previous testimony. Every question has been answered. If we could please move on to something that was not covered yesterday so that the witness does not have to relive the whole testimony of yesterday." Judge Page addressed Mr. Breclaw with, "I certainly don't intend to limit cross-examination, but I have never seen an alleged victim on the stand for three days, for as many days as this alleged victim has been. And I realize that there are many areas to cover, but one of the reasons we might be here so long as we've been is because there are certain areas that are being gone over perhaps unnecessarily often."

Mr. Breclaw took the subtle hint and moved on to a new area. Using a crude drawing of an exam table, lamp, steps, and stirrups, he spent the next 60 questions trying to get Tammy to describe her position on the table in relation to the lamp and paper drape. She couldn't give specific answers and he had trouble wording his questions in such a way that the answers made any sense to the jury.

* * *

Q. "As you were at the end of the table and you were scooted to the end of the table, would it be fair to say that your vagina would be pointed slightly in an upward position?"

A. "I don't understand the question."

Q. "Well, as you're on the table and you've scooted down, your legs are spread, would your vagina be pointed slightly in an upward position?"

A. "What do you mean by pointed? Do you mean like I was up some or do you mean that's the way it's facing. I don't understand what you mean by pointed."

Q.   "Assuming that the table is in this manner (indicating a drawing on the chalk board) and you are scooted down to the end of the table and you're in the stirrups, would your vagina, the canal of your vagina be pointed slightly at an upward angle?"

A.   "I don't know if it would be upward; it would be more like that way [indicating]. It would be more like the front if you're laying down."

Q.   "Didn't you sort of scoot your hips down to the end of the table so that Doctor can get a view of the vaginal area through the speculum?"

A.   "Yes."

Q.   "I'm asking you would it not be a fact that your vagina would be slightly up, maybe at a forty-five degree angle?"

A.   "It's hard to say. I can't see it. How can I tell from back here which way it's pointing. I can't see it."

Q.   "Well, take your time and think about it then, okay?"

A.   "I don't know."

Q.   "How tall is Doctor Koo?"

A.   "I have no idea."

Q.   "Well, give me an approximation."

A.   "I don't know. Five something; that's an approximation. I don't know."

MR. BRECLAW

"Doctor, would you come over here?"

MR. BENSON

"I object, Your Honor."

THE WITNESS

"You put him next to me, I'll slug him."

THE COURT

"Now, you be quiet. This is a court of law and I pointed out yesterday that we settle our disputes peaceably in the courtroom."

THE WITNESS

"I'm sorry. Can I just say there's no way I can tell how tall he is unless he's next to me, and I won't be next to him."

THE COURT

"I understand, and I'm taking that into account. Breclaw, your next question."

MR. BRECLAW

"If I could make an offer to prove, Your Honor?"

THE COURT

"You may ask this witness about defendant's height in relationship to her or as best she can estimate his height, but demonstrative evidence regarding the height of the defendant is inappropriate during the State's case in chief."

* * *

It appeared that the defense was attempting to show that the doctor was too short to be able to stand at the end of the table and physically have intercourse with the plaintiff. Without the actual table and step there was no way of knowing. Maybe there was a point to be made about the relative position of the bodies of the two individuals and the angle of the penis and vagina. But that point was not made during Tammy's testimony, and several jurors were writing questions of their own to hand to the judge.

* * *

Q.   "The unusual feeling that you have testified to pre-
      viously, was that an in-and-out type of feeling?"

A.   "Yes, sir."

Q.   "A feeling that would be like a pushing feeling inside of
      you?"

A.   "In and out."

Q.   "Pushing against the inside of your vagina?"

A.   "Yes, in and out."

Q.   "Is not this the same feeling of a bimanual examination
      that a doctor does with you, pushing and probing the in-
      side of your vagina?"

A.   "No, sir, that is way up and his hands are on your stom-
      ach."

Q.   "When you felt this feeling did the paper rustle?"

A.   "I don't know."

Q.   "Did the paper rustle?"

A.   "I don't know."

Q.   "Had the paper rustled, would you have known it?"

A.   "I don't know."

Q.   "When you felt the in-and-out motion, were you in an
      emotional state of shock?"

A.   "Yes."

Q.   "As you are laying there experiencing this in-and-out
      sensation and in an emotional state of shock as you have
      testified to, in your mind, did this at that time in your
      mind confirm the slight apprehension or fear that you had
      when you went into his office on March 30 that he was
      sexually abusing you or molesting you as he had in a dif-
      ferent manner done on March 14?"

A.   "Yes. Just a little bit. I felt that he was my doctor of 11 years and I trusted him and there had to be a medical reason."

Q.   "Did this confirm in your mind the fears that you had when you went into his office on March 30?"

A.   "That wasn't going through my mind, no."

Q.   "You testified that you didn't kick the doctor in the groin area because you were frozen. Were you in fear of further sexual molestation, of what he was going to do next?"

A.   "I was in a state of shock."

Q.   "Does that include fear?"

A.   "I believe so, yes."

Q.   "You know the difference, do you not, between a man zipping his pants and a man hitching his pants like I'm doing now?"

A.   "Yes, sir."

* * *

The jury was then given an education about how a man zips up his fly. For nine of us it was a waste of time; for the other five it must have been amusing.

Mr. Breclaw then raised the likelihood of Tammy having a yeast infection, and the unlikelihood of a doctor having unprotected sex with a woman he knew to have such an infection. Tammy countered by stating that, even though such infections might be contagious, she had had them before and her husband never got them.

The defense attorney then thanked Tammy for being patient with him during the long cross-examination and told the judge that he had no further questions.

Judge Page then took the written questions he had received from the jurors and addressed them to Tammy.

* * *

THE COURT:

Q. "Do you know how tall Doctor Koo is?"

A. "No, sir."

Q. "Do you know how far the end of the examination table in room number two is from the floor?"

A. "No, sir."

Q. "Can you give any approximation as you would stand next to it how high up on you it would come?"

A. "Around the hip area."

Q. "Would you stand and show the jury how high that is?"

A. "Approximately right here (indicating)."

Q. "Is there a stool in front of the table?"

A. "No, it's at the desk."

Q. "How far is the end of the table from the stool?"

A. "Approximately two feet to the right."

Q. "Where would Doctor Koo's genitals be in comparison to you? And I assume that means when you're on the table and he's standing next to the examination table."

A. "Right in front of me, in my vaginal area."

Q. "Were the doctor's pants down during the alleged act?"

A. "I don't believe so."

Q. "Were you able to see if the pants were down?"

A. "I couldn't really tell, no."

Q. "Do you know if a yeast infection is contagious?"

A. "No, sir, I don't; I don't believe it is."

Q. "Can a man get a yeast infection from a woman during sexual intercourse?"

A.   "My husband has never got it, and we've had sex more than once . . . so to the best of my knowledge, no."

Q.   "Have you had sex with him at times when you have had a yeast infection?"

A.   "Yes, sir; yes, sir."

THE COURT

"Redirect examination, Mr. Benson."

* * *

July 16 • Thursday • late morning

State Attorney Benson conducted his redirect to counter any doubts or false impressions left in the minds of the jurors by Mr. Breclaw's cross-examination.

His first few questions confirmed that Tammy could not tell whether or not the doctor was wearing a condom at the time she glimpsed his penis, nor did he pull the stool up to the exam table. She indicated that the pull-out step was approximately the same height as a normal household stair step. He made the more important points as follows.

* * *

MR. BENSON:

Q.   "Now, yesterday defense counsel had some gloves that he showed you. Do you recall that?"

A.   "Yes."

Q.   "And were those the same as the gloves that you saw the doctor use on previous occasions?"

A.   "I believe he asked me if those were the same color."

Q.   "I would like to show you what's been marked for purposes of identification as State's Exhibit 3 and ask you to please take a look at that. Do you recognize what that is?"

A. "It's an examining glove."

Q. "Now, how does that glove compare with the gloves that Doctor Koo normally wore?"

A. "That's more like it. That's basically the color; that's more like it."

Q. "The one you were shown yesterday, was it a darker color?"

A. "Yes, sir."

Q. "Are you able to distinguish between this glove and what you saw when you caught a glimpse of his penis on March 30?"

A. "Different. No doubt in my mind whatsoever."

Q. "After this incident on March 30, how did you get from the doctor's office to Walgreen's?"

A. "I drove."

Q. "Anyone with you?"

A. "No, sir."

Q. "Whose car was that?"

A. "It was my father's."

Q. "And did you get in any accidents on the way to Walgreen's?"

A. "No, sir."

Q. "Did you have a hard time driving to Walgreen's?"

A. "No, sir."

Q. "Was your driving impaired on the way to Walgreen's?"

A. "No, sir."

Q. "Ms. Garza, is the person that raped you on March 30, 1989, in the courtroom today?"

A. "Yes, sir."

Q. "Will you please tell the ladies and gentlemen of the jury where he is seated and what he is wearing?"

A. "He's seated at the defendant's table in the middle and he's wearing a maroon jacket and blue pants."

THE COURT

"The record will reflect that the witness has identified the defendant before the Court, Young Soo Koo, as the Doctor Koo of whom she speaks."

MR. BENSON

Q. "This occurred at his Kennedy Avenue office in Lake County, Indiana?"

A. "Yes, sir."

MR. BENSON

"Thank you very much, Ms. Garza. No further questions, Your Honor."

* * *

A brief (30 questions) recross-examination by Mr. Breclaw covered some technical details concerning the times noted on Tammy's earlier statements. He indicated he would still need testimony from Tammy during his defense in order to introduce certain prescription records. Judge Page then excused her from the witness box.

Over the three day period Tammy Jane Garza had answered more than 2,230 questions — 570 from Mr. Benson, and more than 1,660 from Mr. Breclaw. Her ordeal over for the time being, she left the witness box and walked into the waiting arms of her husband — head held high, eyes sweeping through the jury box. She had waited three years, three months, and 17 days for this moment — a truly remarkable feat.

A startling change of atmosphere then took place. It was as though a thunderstorm had passed, the skies cleared, and the sun shone brightly. With Tammy's departure had come a relative calm. The courtroom seemed at peace.

5
Balance by Benson

Officially, Philip C. Benson was a Lake County Deputy Prosecutor. He graduated from Valparaiso University Law School in 1989, two months after Tammy's last visit to Dr. Koo. This was his seventh trial as a prosecutor.

By a stroke of good fortune, the Hammond Police Department had given the Dr. Koo investigation to Detective Sergeant Charles (Chuck) Hedinger — 21 years on the force, 10 years dealing with sex crimes.

This partnership was responsible for building a case for prosecution. Not enough evidence wouldn't work; too much would be counterproductive. What was needed was proper balance.

The next witness for the prosecution was Carol Paglis, a pharmacist at Walgreen's in 1989 who had known Tammy and her family for eight years.

She explained the federal regulations for classification and dispensation of controlled substances such as Valium (a schedule IV substance) and codeine (schedule III). The jury learned that doctors authorize refills by marking an appropriate portion of the prescription form — a box for no refills can be checked; a box for refill PRN can be checked; or a circle can be drawn to indicate the exact number of refills, 1-2-3-4-5.

PRN, as Judge Page explained, was Latin for "as the occasion arises" *(pro re nata)*. Federal law allowed five refills in six months for schedule IV items such as Valium. It was not unusual for patients to phone in for a refill and have some other member of the family pick it up.

The heart of Ms. Paglis's testimony was that on her March 30 visit to Walgreen's Tammy was visibly upset — crying and shaking. She was, however, able to stand without weaving and her speech was not slurred. She did not show any signs that would indicate she had taken too much Valium or was going through withdrawal. During his cross-examination of this witness, Mr. Breclaw tried to convince the jury that Tammy's shaking hands were a sign that she was going through some kind of drug withdrawal. Ms. Paglis testified that when Tammy returned later that day her hands were not shaking. She said that Tammy's shaking was more than likely due to her emotional state of mind than in any way connected with drugs.

In response to Mr. Breclaw's question about shaking hands being a symptom of withdrawal she said, "Only if it was like a long-term thing, like if you saw it consistently, but considering her condition — I mean I'm shaking now, and I don't think I'm going through withdrawal."

In his redirect examination Mr. Benson made the point that Tammy was not under the influence of any drug that might have caused her to imagine she had been raped. He next tried to let the jury see that Dr. Koo was prescribing various drugs, Valium and codeine included, in quantities noticeably greater than those prescribed by some 40 doctors Ms. Paglis serviced.

Mr. Breclaw objected and Judge Page sustained the objection.

Outside the hearing of the jury, Mr. Benson argued, "They have battered Ms. Garza up and down about the prescription records and all these drugs she supposedly had taken. She testified that they were all prescribed by the doctor, and it's part of the

State's contention from day one that those prescriptions were written in an attempt to conceal the Valium that was injected on this very day. And this goes to help prove the State's point that that is part of the plan of this defendant to prescribe large amounts of Valium and then when he injects them with Valium at the time of the rape, therefore, it is covered up, and they try to paint this victim as a drug addict."

The judge was not convinced that this was the proper witness for that testimony and he stood by his ruling. Mr. Benson called as his next witness, Tammy's mother Ellen Spasske. Her testimony confirmed Tammy's testimony about the conversation between mother and daughter when Mrs. Spasske felt Dr. Koo could be trusted. She did mention that during her pelvic examinations the doctor had worn the light, cream colored gloves identified by Tammy. Mr. Breclaw's cross-examination was benign.

One point of interest surfaced during her testimony that provided evidence of Mr. Breclaw's inexperience in criminal trial law. When Mr. Benson asked Mrs. Spasske what Dr. Koo had said to her over the phone, Mr. Breclaw objected on the grounds of hearsay. What happened then was an education for the defense.

* * *

THE COURT

"Overruled. The rule of law is that the words of a party opponent are admissible, that the hearsay objection is not available to you when the words of which we speak are those of the defendant."

MR. BRECLAW

"But there are cases where I could not introduce self-serving statements of my client."

THE COURT

"You cannot."

MR. BRECLAW

"He (Mr. Benson) is the only one that can?"

THE COURT

"He is the only one that can. It is a rule peculiar to criminal cases, and what it means is that, generally speaking, the words of another, unless they're a witness on the stand, cannot be brought out. But when it's the defendant in question, because he cannot be compelled to testify under our Constitution, the prosecutor may bring it forward. You, because you have an option (to have the defendant testify or not) may not."

* * *

The next witness for the State was Stanley Spasske, Tammy's father, It seems that Dr. Koo had called Mr. Spasske a couple of days after March 30, 1989, to arrange a meeting in order to deny having raped Tammy. Mr. Spasske called the Hammond police and was advised to meet with the doctor to hear what he had to say. When Mr. Benson got to that point in his questioning, Mr. Breclaw objected to the introduction of Mr. Spasske's statement to the police and the court recessed for the day.

* * *

July 17 • Friday • 9:00 a.m.

Judge Page announced he was taking Mr. Breclaw's objection under advisement. Thus, it was not until Tuesday morning, July 21, that he read the statement to the jury and allowed the testimony of Tammy's father to continue.

Mr. Spasske's statement, dated May 9, 1989, read as follows:

"Dr. Koo left a message with my other daughter, Becky, on April 1 to meet him at Freddy's Steak House at 6:00 p.m. I went there and Dr. Koo and I talked. He told me he wanted to talk to me 'father to father,' and he said he couldn't do it because he has had sexual problems for the last five years. He said he would try but couldn't do it. He wanted to go across the street to his office to prove that he couldn't have done it. I asked him how, and he said let's go, and we went to his office. He showed me how she was on the table and because of how short he was he couldn't reach her. Then he wanted to show me his penis to prove that it wasn't big enough to penetrate anyone, but I told him I didn't want to see it. That's about it. Then we left his office and we went to a tavern called Brothers Two, and he kept repeating about not being able to do it and about his sexual problems that he had had for the past five years."

Judge Page did not read, and the jury never heard, one sentence in Stanley's statement that went, "He said that's why his wife left him and that he was now living with his receptionist and that he still couldn't make it."

Mr. Benson asked Mr. Spasske only one question after the statement had been read. It was, "When you were at the doctor's office on that night after you left Freddy's Steak House, did he pull the step out from the examining table for you?"

Mr. Spasske responded, "No, he did not."

A few days after that meeting Dr. Koo had written a letter to Mr. Spasske that was placed in evidence. It read as follows.

Dear Stanley,

I had to write this letter to you. I am so disappointed about the story.

I have not done anything wrong to my patient for past 11 years and I tried my best to help my patients. Therefore all patients are loyal to me and I respect them too.

I love Ellen and you, so I tried to take care of your kids too, but I do not want to hear bad thing. As I told you, I want Tammy has a job to get out of headaches and depression, so she is able to pursue her life better, but since she is telling like that, I gave up on everything and I will not discuss about her anymore.

I thought she was acted by shot and might be illusion reaction. I have nothing to hide because I've never dreamed about it. I want Tammy come to see me and see the fact whether I am or anybody is able to do so in such conditions and such high exam table. Like I said, if I could, I am more happy than anybody. Why? I explained to you, that I have had problem with sexuality for past five years. I am thinking myself how I am able to function at anytime, and also you better ask Beverly the fact of my problem. We tried to make love, but failed because of me. This is second time I am addressing you that you can accuse me everything but not sex.

This is going to drop my reputation, if she want, tell her go ahead. I want to keep relationship with you and Ellen as usual. That all I hope, because I care about you and Ellen.

Sincerely,
(signed) Young Koo

After a midmorning break Mr. Benson called his next witness, Karen Anderson, a fully qualified emergency room nurse who was on duty at St. Margaret's Hospital when Tammy was examined on the evening of March 30, 1989. Under direct examination her testimony was essentially as follows.

"The sexual assault kit is just a box. The police department issues them to hospitals. They are sealed kits, and you open them and there is a paper inside that explains all the tests that they want done, and it's the kit for evidence for the police. That's what we explain to the patient, and we get blood tests, we get hair specimens from them, pubic hair and head hair, swabs of their mouth, vagina, rectum, whatever is pertinent to that case, wherever they were raped.

"The physician does the pelvic exam, and then we get the specimens that way.

"Tammy came into the emergency room and said that she had been sexually assaulted. She was straightforward and alert and told me her story and we did our exam. First we do a blood pressure and vital signs, ask her her medical history, is she allergic to anything, take any medicine, that kind of thing.

"From the emergency room report I have here, her blood pressure was 100 over 50 — normal. I also noted on this report at the time of the exam that 'she was conscious; she was alert; she was warm, dry. Her color was good. I noted a puncture wound to right antecubital site (inside arm, just below elbow joint, where shots are normally given intravenously).

"Intravenous means the shot goes right into the blood system, into the vein, and it hits you right away. Intramuscular (as in the hip or buttocks area) goes into a muscle, so it's absorbed slowly through your system. Like a tetanus shot would go in your arm. If you had a shot for pain, it usually goes in the hip.

"Dr. Rane did the pelvic exam on Tammy. He did not give her any injections beforehand. I did not note any sign that Tammy was going through Valium or codeine withdrawal."

Mr. Benson had Ms. Anderson state that the normal dimensions of the exam table used for testing rape victims at St. Margaret's were four feet long and two and a half feet wide, with stirrups that pull out. She didn't know the exact height but did offer that most exam tables were of the same height and contained a step at the stirrup end.

After the usual legal two-step, Mr. Breclaw stipulated that Dr. Koo was five-foot, five-inches tall. The judge had the doctor stand in the middle of the court and Ms. Anderson left the witness box to stand alongside him to better observe his height.

She was then able to answer that if an individual of the doctor's height were standing on the exam table step, his genitals would be "pretty close" to those of a woman on the table in the examination position. She testified that, under those conditions, sexual intercourse would be possible.

Mr. Benson then placed into evidence the actual, sealed rape kit that contained the specimens from Tammy's examination. He asked the witness to tell the jury what was in the kit. Ms. Anderson cut the seal and noted the following.

"There is paper with instructions. There are vaginal and cervical swabs from the pelvic exam — two separate Q-tips. The two glass slides contain the two smears. This is the vaginal wash — how they get the semen specimens. We take a syringe with maybe ten or twenty cc's of water, and we actually squirt it into her vagina and then suck it out and it goes in a test tube for a semen test. These are 40 to 50 head and pubic hairs that we pulled out by the roots. This is where we took a saliva test — put this half moon disk in her mouth and mark where it becomes stained and let it air dry.

"This is her blood sample. Everything is labeled and I had to sign my name and put her name and initial everything that I did. And then these are her underpants. She hadn't changed her clothes so we saved the underpants. And on the paper we complete the information — who the doctor was, who collected, who witnessed the collection, and that was me, and afterwards, after you put all the specimens in, you seal it up. There are these red tapes, and you seal up the kit until the police pick it up."

Mr. Benson asked her to consider the height of the doctor and the dimensions of the table and step. He then asked his final question, "Would the genitals of each individual be such in line that sexual intercourse would be possible?"

She answered, "I would think so. Yes, I think so."

July 17 • Friday • 1:30 p.m.

Under Mr. Breclaw's cross-examination Ms. Anderson described the collection of the urine sample as, "The sample kit comes in a plastic baggie, and there is a cup, a sterile cup with a lid on it, and there are three little towelettes for cleaning yourself in a package, and you tell them to go to the bathroom, and they open up the towelettes, and they need to wipe themselves clean three times with each of the towelettes before they urinate in the toilet. Then they stop; then they urinate in the cup; and then they finish in the toilet. So it's called a clean catch midstream urine specimen, and then you put the sterile lid back on it and then we label it."

Chain of Custody

The subject of "chain of custody" came up and Judge Page clarified this matter for the jury, "Ladies and gentlemen of the jury, you've heard the term chain of custody used, and I have reason to believe you may hear more of that term in the days or weeks to come. When an item is taken and one can't tell by looking at it where it came from, we call that in law an item that must be specifically identified. What attorneys have to do, if they wish to use evidence of tests that are performed on those items, is clearly connect them with the subject in question. Before the results of any sample can come in, it must be clear enough for you to reasonably conclude that the sample came from the patient in question.

"For example, a nurse might collect a sample from a patient, label it, personally take it to a locked storage area, retrieve it later, take it to a lab and witness it signed into the lab. After the nurse so testified, the lab technician would then testify as to the item's receipt and subsequent analysis."

Ms. Anderson's testimony established her part in the chain of custody for the items in the rape kit, but raised a serious question about the chain for Tammy's urine sample. Later in the trial the chain of custody was established for the rape kit items and they were admitted into evidence.

But subsequent testimony by Regina Heilman, the nurse who collected Tammy's urine sample, indicated that she did not follow proper procedure. She had left the cup containing Tammy's urine in an unlocked and unattended storage area where, eventually, Karen Anderson picked it up and took it to the lab.

This gap in the chain, while somewhat innocuous, did make it possible for someone to have tampered with the sample while no one was around. For that reason there was a question as to its admissibility.

It ended as a "much ado about nothing" thing because both Mr. Breclaw and Mr. Benson wanted to use the urine test results (medium to high levels of Valium and codeine), each for his own reason, and they agreed to accept same as coming from Tammy's specimen. The court allowed this stipulation because the jury was aware of the gap and could place whatever weight they wished on the testimony and counsels' remarks concerning the results. Dr. Shashikant Rane was the next witness for the State. Mr. Benson identified him as trained for internal medicine and board certified for emergency room medicine. He had examined Tammy and taken the rape kit specimens. The State's questions were few and to the point.

* * *

Q.   "Is there anyone else present in the room?"

A.   "Invariably a nurse is present at the time of the examination."

Q.   "And why is that?"

A.   "One thing, to assist with the examination, and second, if I'm examining a victim who is alleging sexual assault, I want to protect myself with a third party in the room."

Q.   "What exactly do you do in relation to this exam?"

A. "Once the patient is placed in the position then you first do an external examination of the vaginal area to see if there are any bruises, any kind of injury. After that a speculum is inserted into the vagina, which is opened up to see the inside of the vagina, and I would collect some specimens from the inside of the vagina for the rape kit. After that is done I would do a bimanual examination, when I insert two of my gloved fingers inside of the vagina to feel if there is any tenderness, pain or other kind of injury or any masses in the vagina. For the bimanual pelvic examination you have to stand on the right side of the patient so that you can insert two fingers in the vagina and you can feel your other hand on the uterus from above. Most of the time it is done standing up."

Q. "Does the bimanual exam involve an in and out motion repeatedly with your hands?"

A. "No."

Q. "What is a speculum and what does it look like?"

A. "It is an instrument that when you insert it into the vagina, it is flat, but you have a lever at the other end which you press, and the speculum will open up exposing the uterus inside."

Q. "You don't push the speculum back and forth once it's in there?"

A. "No, you don't."

Q. "Do you use any kind of motions with your hand during the bimanual exam or the speculum that could be confused with sex, sexual intercourse, the back and forth motion?"

A. "No, because you put in the speculum and open it up and it gets locked. You finish your examination, and once you unlock the speculum, it will come out. When you are doing a bimanual examination, you just go in one time and you just start to feel the inside of the pelvis with your fingers."

Q. "Do you do anything prior to a pelvic exam that involves the use of drugs?"

A. "No."

Q. "Did you observe any puncture wounds on Ms. Spasske?"

A. "I did notice one puncture on the right antecubital fossa, which is this area [indicating forearm]."

Q. "And you made a visual inspection of Ms. Spasske's vagina?"

A. "Yes, I did."

Q. "And did you notice any boils in that area?"

A. "I do not recall seeing any boils, neither does the medical records that I made and which I have reviewed specify anything about that, so I don't think so."

Q. "Is that something you would have listed had you seen that?"

A. "Absolutely."

Q. "Doctor, if a boil was there, would you have seen it?"

A. "Yes, positively."

* * *

During Mr. Breclaw's cross-examination the jury learned that only water is used to wet the speculum before use. Lubricants can contaminate whatever cultures are taken. Nor is K-Y jelly used to lubricate the lips of the vagina prior to use of the speculum. It is used to lubricate the latex glove for the bimanual portion of the examination. Dr. Rane could think of no medical reason that would explain Tammy's testimony concerning Dr. Koo's fingers moving around the lips of her vagina.

There then followed a long and fruitless series of questions and answers concerning the angle of the vagina in relation to the position of the patient with her feet in the stirrups. The basic problem was Mr. Breclaw's lack of understanding about the subject and thus his inability to ask the proper questions. Finally, an exasperated Dr. Rane gave the entire courtroom a brief lesson in the female anatomy.

"Yes, there is a slight tilt of the vagina upward but that is not why I insert my fingers down. I insert them down because I am tall, and the patient is at the lower level. I'm sorry, it is not to be in line with the vagina, no. It doesn't matter which angle you go into the vagina. You can go in any angle in the vagina. You can go in the cavity. It's an empty space. The vagina is collapsed until you put a speculum in there and open it up. It is not a rigid structure. It's a skin flap. I don't know if it's going to satisfy you, but even if the length of the vagina in a woman five feet tall is four inches, maybe more in a taller woman, a doctor can use two inches of his fingers to reach the organs he's examining. Those internal organs hang from ligaments and are suspended in the pelvis. It doesn't matter whether the patient is seven feet tall or three feet tall, you can reach the internal organs which are fixed in the pelvis. You have somebody who is three hundred or four hundred pounds, that is the only patient you will have trouble doing a pelvic exam. You don't feel the vagina; you feel the organs inside. In an average woman a doctor should be able to feel the organs with his fingers up to just here (indicating two inches). You first move your fingers to the right to touch the right ovary, then to the middle to touch the uterus, then to the left to touch the left ovary. It normally takes one minute and does not involve an in-and-out movement, although some in-and-out movement is possible. Also, the standard height of the exam table throughout this area is three feet. All the tables are fixed concerning height and most have a step at one end. While Valium can be used as a tranquilizer to relax a tense patient, I have never used Valium for that purpose."

Mr. Benson's redirect covered two points (Mr. Breclaw having stipulated Dr. Koo's height).

* * *

Q. "If a man five-foot, five-inches tall were standing on the exam table step and a woman was in position for a pelvic exam, based upon your knowledge and experience of the male body and the female anatomy, would it be physically possible for sexual intercourse to occur?"

A. "It is possible."

Q. "Is there anything about the angle of the vagina that would prohibit that from occurring?"

A. "No."

Q. "Could an individual have a medium to high level of codeine and Valium, as determined by urine analysis, and still be completely oriented as to time and space?"

A. "Yes, it's possible, yes."

* * *

Judge Page then reviewed the questions for the witness that came from individual members of the jury. With the agreement of both attorneys, he read them to Dr. Rane as follows.

* * *

Q. "Doctor, during a bimanual pelvic exam, is the doctor standing between the patients legs?"

A. "It can be done between the patient's legs, but the preferable position is, if the doctor is right-handed, he will stand on the right side of the patient. If the doctor is left-handed, he will be more comfortable with the left side of the patient."

Q. "Do you stand completely to the right side of the patient where you would be completely seen on a bimanual exam?"

A. "Yes."

Q. "At which point of the exam does the doctor do a visual exam, before or after the speculum?"

A. "The visual exam is really done at two stages. Before you enter with the speculum, you look at the vagina from outside, and once you insert the speculum inside, you open it up and visually inspect how the cervix looks. The cervix is the lower portion of the uterus."

Q. "Is the speculum always removed for a bimanual pelvic exam?"

A. "Yes, absolutely."

Q. "Will a visual exam of the vaginal area reveal a boil that was lanced recently?"

A. "Absolutely, yes."

* * *

July 17 • Friday • late afternoon

The next witness for the prosecution was Kim Epperson, a forensic DNA analyst and forensic serologist. She was accepted by the court as an expert witness who was qualified to give legal (forensic) evidence concerning the testing and test result interpretation of human body fluids (serology) — typically blood, seminal fluid, perspiration, and saliva. She was employed at the Indiana State Police laboratory in Indianapolis and had tested Tammy's samples from the rape kit.

July 20 • Monday • 9 a.m.

Ms. Epperson answered Mr. Benson's questions as follows.

"The first test that I run is for the presence of acid phosphatase, an enzyme that is secreted by the prostate (male only) gland. It contributes a large amount of fluid into seminal fluid. Seminal fluid is basically made up of two components, secretions from the prostate gland and secretions from the seminal vesicles. Acid phosphatase is an enzyme that is found in very high concentrations in seminal fluid — twenty to four hundred times greater than it is found in other body fluids. But because this enzyme, acid phosphatase, is also found in other body fluids, we can only use this test as a screening test or what we call a presumptive test.

"A presumptive test is a test that indicates the substance might be seminal fluid, but does not confirm it. I need to go on and perform additional tests in order to confirm or in order to be able to say with one hundred percent certainty the substance that I found is seminal fluid. We do two confirmatory tests in our laboratory.

"The first one is the P-30 test, and P-30 is a semen specific protein. What that means is the only place in the human body that P-30 has been found is in males and in seminal fluid. So if I get a positive reaction on the P-30 test, I confirm or I conclusively say that seminal fluid is present.

"We also do a second confirmatory test, and that's a test for the presence of spermatozoa. Spermatozoa or sperm cells are the male reproductive cells. Again the only place they're found in the human body naturally occurring is in males and in seminal fluid. So with either the P-30 or the sperm cells or a combination of the two I can confirm that seminal fluid is present.

"There is a reason that we do both tests. There are individuals who have a very low sperm count or who have been vasectomized that won't show sperm cells in their seminal fluid, but they will still have the acid phosphatase and the P-30, so we routinely do a series of three tests.

"The first test for acid phosphatase is a chemical test. It's a real simple color change test. We take a small portion of the area we think is stained with seminal fluid. For example, on the underpants, I would cut out a real small square of the material where seminal fluid might be. I put that material in a test tube, and I add a mixture of chemicals to that test tube, and then I incubate the tube or put it in an oven for thirty minutes. I take it out of the oven and add a second set of chemicals, and when I have a blue color, I have a positive reaction. We grade our acid phosphatase reaction. A strong positive reaction, a dark blue color, is graded as four plus, and then we go down the scale. Three plus is a little weaker; two plus is weaker yet; and one plus is the weakest positive reaction, and then there would be a negative. A negative is a yellow color.

"Any time I get a positive reaction of any level I go ahead and run the two confirmatory tests.

"The P-30 test is what we call an immunological reaction. A positive reaction results in a white precipitin band I can visually see with my eyes. The sperm test is simply microscopic.

I look for sperm cells on a glass slide under a microscope.

"I tested the following items from Ms. Spasske's rape kit: A) vaginal swabs; B) cervical swabs; C) smear slides from both swabs; D) vaginal wash; and E) underpants." The vaginal and cervical swabs both yielded the same result. For the acid phosphatase test both swabs gave a one plus reaction, and they were negative for P-30 and sperm.

"Smear slides can only be tested for sperm; both were tested and both found to be negative.

"On the vaginal wash, which is a tube of liquid, I did the acid phosphatase test. It was negative. I did not do the P-30 test because it was liquid. I did do the sperm test; it, too, was negative.

"Now, the dilution effect of the saline (vaginal) wash makes it very hard to detect acid phosphatase.

"On the underpants I tested five areas. Normally what I do with a pair of underpants is I visually examine them and look for stains on the entire area of the underpants. Also, unless the underpants are white, I can do an ultraviolet light test. In this case the underpants were white in color, so I was not able to do that test. What I did was I visually examined the item and I determined that the crotch area of the underpants was stained. It was stained a light yellow color, and it had a black dirt like streak across the back, so what I did is I wanted to test those areas that appeared yellowish, so on the panties, the crotch area has a seam in the front or towards the stomach as you would wear them and a seam in the back or towards the rear. In this case I took five samples, number one being at the front, two, three, four, and five closest to the rear. I cut out a small square of the fabric to do the testing.

"Number one, the area closest to the front, was negative. There was no acid phosphatase present there. Number two and number three I got a two plus reading for acid phosphatase. Number four I got a three plus reading for acid phosphatase, and number five, closest to the back, was negative. I tested all three for sperm and for P-30 with negative results on all three cuttings.

"I would say from my experience at least 50 percent of the time when I have a three plus reaction I will also have a positive reaction for sperm and P-30.

"There are substances other than seminal fluid that can give a weak reading for acid phosphatase. I would not expect any of these other substances to give me a four plus reading. I would also find it unusual to get a three plus reading on one of these other substances.

"The substance in the body that has the closest level of acid phosphatase to that of seminal fluid is menstrual blood. Menstrual blood has acid phosphatase present in a concentration about twenty times less than that of seminal fluid, so it's the closest one of all the other body fluids.

"There are certain other things, for example, if a woman should have a vaginal infection where she might have a high concentration of bacteria in the vaginal cavity, those bacteria can give a weak positive acid phosphatase level, usually about a one plus, remotely a two plus.

"Some other things that might give a weak positive acid phosphatase level would be fecal material which would give a one plus. Horseradish juice or cabbage juice, if poured directly on the material, could give a one plus. However, in this case, there was no blood present, and I also did not detect any fecal material.

"There are basically three reasons that might lead to a positive acid phosphatase but a negative test for P-30 and sperm. One would be that the individual waited a long time before testing — up to 72 hours. The P-30 and the sperm might be gone; however, you could still detect an acid phosphatase level because that's a very sensitive test. I say 72 hours because studies have shown that to be the maximum amount of time that seminal fluid can survive in the victim's body cavity.

"The second reason I might only detect acid phosphatase and none of the other components of seminal fluid would be if the victim cleaned up in some manner — if she douched, if she showered, bathed, scrubbed the vaginal area — that's going to remove a great majority of the body fluid, of the seminal fluid that might be present. However, some of the acid phosphatase might remain to be found by this very sensitive test.

"The third reason I might only detect acid phosphatase and not P-30 or sperm would be that perhaps there was no ejaculation. There is a substance that's called preejaculatory fluid. When a male is in an erect condition, when he's in a sexually excited state, a little bubble of fluid forms at the end of the male sex organ that is called preejaculatory fluid. It's just a bubble, maybe the amount is the size of the tip of your finger. That little bubble of fluid contains all of the components of seminal fluid. It contains acid phosphatase, P-30, and sperm. Because it's such a small amount the likelihood is if you're going to detect anything from preejaculatory fluid, it would probably only be the acid phosphatase.

"I would expect preejaculatory fluid to test anywhere from one plus to three plus. I would probably not find a four plus.

"Since I did not find sperm, I could not do DNA testing. In order to do DNA testing you need sperm cells present.

"Now, if there is a vaginal infection, yeast or otherwise, I usually find a wide, thick, crusty stain on the swabs and the underpants. In this case I found no evidence of any vaginal infection."

Mr. Benson then presented Tammy's story (no ejaculation, cleaned out with some kind of swab, and tested three hours later) as a hypothetical case and asked Ms. Epperson if her test results would be consistent with an incident like that. She answered that they would be — that she would only detect acid phosphatase. She added that a three plus level of acid phosphatase would be more typical of seminal fluid than any other of the items she had discussed.

The cross-examination was conducted by Mr. Binder. Since she held to her testimony, he was left with the sole alternative of sexual intercourse with someone else within the 72-hour window before the rape kit samples were taken.

July 20 • Monday • late afternoon

Phil Benson then called another expert witness, Lisa Black, a hair analyst with the Indiana State Police. This was actually a negative type of testimony since no hairs of Mongoloid (Asian) origin were found when Tammy's pubic area was combed.

Rather than have the defense contend that the absence of Mongoloid hairs was evidence that Dr. Koo was innocent, Benson called Lisa to testify that such hair transfers are rare. In her personal experience they occurred less than 10 percent of the time — the literature mentioned 3 to 4 percent.

Late Monday and early Tuesday the State presented testimony from three witnesses: the pharmacist supervisor from Walgreen's, the pharmacist from Fairmeadows Pharmacy, and a technician from Walgreen's. Their testimony merely confirmed the testimony of previous witnesses.

Mr. Benson's last witness for the prosecution was the social worker from Haven House who testified as to Tammy's mental state after the rape.

He wanted to call additional witnesses but the judge had not yet ruled on the admissibility of their evidence. As such, the State indicated it was finished presenting evidence unless, and until, the testimony of the additional witnesses was ruled admissible.

Judge Page instructed Mr. Breclaw to call his first witness for the defense.

6
Fact or Fantasy?

July 21 • Tuesday • early afternoon

Mr. Breclaw called Daniel Zurawski, the pharmacist from Fairmeadows Pharmacy, as the first witness for the defense and had him testify about the number of prescriptions he had filled for Tammy and the frequency of their refills.

This testimony carried over to Wednesday morning as the jury was exposed to a line by line admission into evidence of every prescription ever written for Tammy and her family for the past several years. It was total overkill.

His second witness covered the medical records from St. Margaret's Hospital so that Tammy's visit and her test results could be admitted into evidence. The nurse who took Tammy's urine specimen testified next. From both we learned of two interesting failures on the part of the staff and management of St. Margaret's.

The first, suspected earlier in the trial and now confirmed, was that Tammy's urine sample had been left unattended in an unlocked storage room — breaking the "chain of evidence" and casting doubt as to the origin of the urine tested.

The second failure involved the paper work required for any sexual assault incident. When a patient was admitted for an alleged rape, the admitting nurse took down the information, placing each detail in its proper box. Since there was a box for the name of the alleged rapist, if known, Tammy's form displayed the name of Dr. Koo in said box.

Farther down the form was a box for the name of the victim's physician. And, sure enough, Tammy's report displayed the name of Dr. Koo there as well.

The admitting nurse then passed both Tammy and the form on to the nurse who handled the actual rape kit examination. She completed the form and, following the instructions printed at its end, called Dr. Koo's office to notify him that one of his patients, Tammy Spasske, had been examined for sexual assault.

Anyone familiar with hospital protocol knows that a doctor on the staff of a hospital has unrestricted access to anything he wants anywhere within the hospital — samples, test results, records — anything.

Needless to say, Dr. Young Soo Koo was on the staff of St. Margaret's Hospital. There is no evidence that Dr. Koo came to the hospital, but he could have. He was also informed of police involvement which gave him the opportunity to dispose of any and all physical evidence.

Mr. Breclaw's next witness was a doctor from Valparaiso, Indiana, who testified about standard medical practices in the area. We learned that, while some of Dr. Koo's practices (taping the paper drape to the lamp, standing between a patient's legs during a bimanual exam, and injecting a patient with Valium prior to a pelvic exam) were a bit out of the ordinary (the word "rare" came up several times), they did not violate the boundaries of standard medical practice.

The chemist who analyzed Tammy's urine was next. We learned officially what we had already heard — her urine tested medium to high for codeine and Valium. Evidently Tammy had been taking the codeine prescribed by Dr. Koo. And, of course, there was no mystery where the Valium came from.

Counsel for the defense was now ready to present his star witness to support the principal pillar of his defense — Dr. Hector Carlos Sabelli. Doctor Sabelli informed the jury that he was both a psychiatrist and a pharmacologist as well as a professor of pharmacology and an associate professor of psychiatry at Rush University, an M.D. and a Ph.D. in pharmacology, and board certified in psychiatry and neurology. He was licensed to practice medicine in Illinois and did so at Rush-Presbyterian-St. Luke Hospital with a group of physicians calling themselves the Midwest Neuropsychiatric Association.

He noted that Rush University was connected to the hospital and included a medical school, nursing school, and various graduate schools. He had been a professor of pharmacology at Rush since 1984. As an afterthought he mentioned receiving an award in biological psychiatry in 1963 as well as a number of other awards from various institutions in the course of many years. Judge Page didn't think it necessary to clutter up the court records with 30 pages of additional credentials.

As I sat in the jury box and listened to the recitation of Dr. Sabelli's qualifications and accomplishments the alarm bells began going off in my head.

While working as a metallurgist in the steel industry I had personally experienced many situations where well-qualified metallurgists made mistakes when the subject drifted away from their areas of expertise. Technology has become so complex that it's difficult to keep up to date in one's specialty, let alone one's general field.

Even the experts are human. And humans have egos. I wondered if this expert would testify in areas outside his specialty rather than admit in court that he didn't know the answer or was not qualified to comment.

Dr. Sabelli's area of expertise involved the use of drugs in the treatment of mental and emotional disorders. He claimed no special knowledge in the use of drugs to treat physical disorder.

What follows are the essential portions of his testimony.

* * *

Q.   "Is the drug Valium addictive?"

A.   "Yes. Addiction is the abuse of a drug which is linked to the presence of withdrawal symptoms. When the person stops taking the drug, he or she experiences something missing which is unpleasant."

Q.   "Can you give an example of a situationally-induced hallucination?"

A.   "There are a number of cases that have been documented in which people under anesthesia have experienced and have reported sexual fantasies in which they have come to court and accused physicians or dentists of sexual abuse. And there have been witnesses at the scene who could testify that this was not the case. Anesthetics that have been so involved are diazepam (trade named Valium) and derivatives of diazepam."

Q.   "Assume that a female who on March 14 has a concern that her physician during a pelvic examination had entered into foreplay with her, and that further, on March 30 that this female went back to the physician and was mildly concerned with the situation that she perceived as occurring on March 14, would this female be in a mental state receptive to experience a situationally-induced hallucination during a pelvic exam with that physician?"

A.   "You're asking two different questions from my point of view. From the psychiatric viewpoint, if a person is in the frame of mind having sexual connotations in the past, it seems to me that it's more likely that this time whatever happens will tend to have more sexual connotations. That's the psychiatric part, independent of the drugs. As for the drugs, codeine can produce hallucinations, but that is not common with regular adults. Valium can produce hallucinations, again not a common thing. When one has a combination of drugs, now the story is very different because what happens when one has two drugs affecting the brain is a very, very difficult thing to know. The psychological situation may influence in what direction a person may have an interpretation or a hallucination. The drugs themselves combine to produce a certain clouding of the mind and may produce hallucinations by themselves. There could be a potentiation where you have a greater effect or a different effect with a combination of the two drugs as contrasted to the administration of each of them separately."

Q.   "Is a sexual fantasy, is that a hallucination?"

A.   "A hallucination may include a sexual component, yes." People can have sexual fantasies without hallucinating."

Q.   "What is a sexual fantasy?"

THE COURT

"It's the afternoon again."

MR. BRECLAW

Q.   "Could you describe for us what a sexual fantasy is in relation to a hallucination, or don't you want to touch that one?"

THE COURT

"We could break early."

THE WITNESS

A.   "I think we're having trouble here. More properly speaking, these would be sexual hallucinations. Okay, yes, during the course of hallucinations one can have sexual hallucinations. This can be tactile (touching) as well as visual (seeing) as well as auditory (hearing), and the person may be very difficult to be convinced that this is not true."

Q.   "Having reviewed the prescription records of Fairmeadows Pharmacy with respect to codeine and Valium prescribed for Tammy Spasske, if she ingested as prescribed, do you have an opinion as to whether or not she is a drug abuser?"

A.   "No, I do not. If the person has a very severe pain, maybe it is all right that these drugs be so prescribed. If a person does not have a pain level and level of anxiety that justifies this, this is a very high level of drugs, and it may be that this person is abusing drugs, yes. A person may because of medical illness, because of levels of pain, be required to take very large amounts of medication. This person is not abusing drugs, he or she is using drugs for a medical purpose as prescribed by a doctor and under the doctor's control. However, the person still will be addicted because of, you know, the use of the drug has a physiological effect on the body that will produce addiction."

* * *

Mr. Breclaw asked Dr. Sabelli to consider the rate at which the prescriptions were filled by Fairmeadows Pharmacy and offer his opinion about the condition of a person taking the quantities indicated (these quantities were two to three times greater than Tammy had testified to actually taking). The doctor testified that such a person would be addicted to both codeine and Valium if they took such quantities. He further testified that withdrawal symptoms would occur if the person stopped taking either drug for a period of 48 hours. He noted the withdrawal symptoms of Valium as tremors, shaking, and even seizures — all made worse than normal by the presence of codeine in the system. Mr. Breclaw then passed the witness to Mr. Benson for cross-examination.

* * *

MR. BENSON:

Q. "You described the withdrawal symptoms for Valium for a person taking quantities noted on the pharmacy record. What about codeine withdrawal symptoms?"

A. "With codeine there will probably be emotional symptoms at the beginning and there may be other things like sweating or itching or changes in blood pressure, changes in respiration, weight."

Q. "Would it be fair to say that people build up a tolerance to these drugs — Valium and codeine?"

A. "Yes."

Q. "Would it be fair to say that side effects like hallucinations are very, very rare?"

A. "Hallucinations are very rare in the typical medical use of those drugs; however, hallucinations are extremely common in the surgical use of the drugs because the circumstances are different. The dosages are higher and the persons have more drugs in their body. The patient that comes to an office and you give a prescription, that's a medical use of the drug — the person goes home and takes it. Usually the doses are lower, and it's taken orally. A person undergoing surgery or a person in an intensive care unit because of a heart attack, maybe as many as 30, 40, 50 percent have hallucinations."

Q. "You were given a hypothetical question by defense counsel if a person went to their doctor and felt that some type of foreplay might have occurred and if they went back to the physician with these concerns in the back of

their mind, would they be likely to have a sexual hallucination, and what was your answer to that?"

A.   "Yes."

Q.   "Would it make a difference if part of that hypothetical
was that this person had been their family physician for
10 years and they had trusted him, and returned because
they thought nothing wrong had occurred?"

A.   "Yes."

Q.   "Now, doctor, you mentioned that you're aware of some
studies or some literature that you read about some potential for these types of sexual hallucinations, is that correct?"

A.   "Yes."

Q.   "And it's very fair to say that this phenomena of hallucination is very, very rare?"

A.   "It's a rare thing, yes."

Q.   "Are you aware of how many Valium prescriptions have
been written in the last 10 years?"

A.   "It varies from year to year, but there have been mil-
lions."

Q.   "And I believe you had testified previously that you're
aware of maybe 10 to 20 situations where a sexually-in-
duced hallucination occurred as a result of Valium?"

A.   "Yes, that I'm aware of personally, yes."

MR. BENSON

"Thank you very much, Doctor."

THE COURT

"Redirect examination. Excuse me, Mr. Bailiff? [The bailiff
hands two written questions from the jury to the judge.] Counsel?"

OUTSIDE THE HEARING OF THE JURY

THE COURT

"I don't know, maybe the juror is seeking medical advice. I can't tell. 'Do you agree that the use of drugs in strong and frequent doses for relief from extreme pain, as in treatment of wounds received in military combat situations, is much less likely to result in addiction or hallucination than if taken for reasons other than extreme pain?' "

MR. BRECLAW

"It's a combination of the drugs in this case, Valium and codeine. I would object to that question being asked."

THE COURT

"On what basis is your objection, Mr. Benson?"

BY MR. BENSON

"I believe it's confusing and partially irrelevant, and it is a different situation, hypothetical, that's not applicable here."

THE COURT

"I understand what's being asked. Do you gentlemen see it?"

MR. BENSON

"Frankly, no."

THE COURT

"Basically what it's asking, what has been said by the doctor is that the taking of large quantities of drugs that act on the central nervous system does make it more likely that hallucinations or addiction will result. What this person is asking is that if it's being taken in this case for pain, if it's actually treating something that's

wrong with the body, rather than just being taken by a normal body
— you see it in that context?

* * *

After more discussion, which included the other question from
the jury, Judge Page decided to allow both questions to be asked of
the witness.

As for myself, I found it most fascinating to read, a year and a
half after the trial, the transcripts of what I had not been able to
hear while sitting in the jury box. For the question was mine. And
the judge, to his credit, understood what was being asked. He did
not, however, have a clue as to why the question was asked. I already knew the answer. I had asked the question to see if Dr. Sabelli would testify correctly about something that was outside his
area of expertise.

For years I had been aware that thousands of soldiers had been
treated with morphine to relieve pain resulting from combat
wounds. I had received morphine myself when wounded in Korea,
as did many of my friends. When the pain stopped so did the shots.

I do not recall a single case of addiction or withdrawal symptoms that resulted from morphine given under those conditions. I
never knew why until two years before the trial.

On the cover of the February issue of "Scientific American"
was a promotional phrase that read, "Why morphine taken for
pain is not addictive." The article on page 27 was written by
Ronald Melzack, who had been studying the neurophysiology of
pain for 35 years. He was a professor of psychology at McGill University and research director of the Pain Clinic at Montreal General
Hospital. While on the faculty of the Massachusetts Institute of
Technology he and Patrick Wall, a Ph.D. in psychology, began to
develop their now famous "gate control" theory of pain.

The article went into great technical detail about the body
mechanisms involved, and provided me with an answer that had

eluded me for years. His basic position is that morphine (and codeine is essentially a weaker form of morphine) taken for pain will not cause addiction or withdrawal symptoms unless the patient has a prior history of drug abuse. He cited several studies involving thousands of patients.

* * *

WITHIN THE HEARING OF THE COURT

THE COURT

Q. "Do you agree that the use of drugs in strong and frequent doses for relief from extreme pain, as in the treatment of wounds received in military combat situations, is much less likely to result in addiction or hallucination than if they are taken for reasons other than extreme pain?"

THE WITNESS

A. "There are two questions here for me. One is addiction and the other is hallucination. As far as the addiction is concerned, the person who receives a drug will become addicted most likely, regardless of what is the reason why the person is receiving the drug. For instance, in the treatment of cancer patients, very likely a cancer patient treated with opiates (morphine or codeine) will become addicted to the opiate, and this will happen because this is the nature of the biological interaction between the drug and the body.

"On the other hand, with respect to the production of abnormal psychological symptoms, such as maybe a hallucination or something like that, one tends to observe them more in the case of a person who has other reasons, emotional dysfunctions and so on to use the drug, abuse the drug. First of all, because to begin with there is something abnormal psychologically and maybe even in the biology of this person. Point number two, because they don't tend to take one drug, but they tend to take several. Nevertheless, the experience is that even people who receive drugs for legitimate reasons can have a number of side effects of a psychological nature."

It appeared to me that this expert witness had fallen into the "expert-witness trap." He testified in an area outside his specialty in a situation in which he was unqualified. The good Dr. Sabelli was still in the pre-1980 era (studies cited were published in 1980) when most doctors were concerned about patients becoming addicted to drugs prescribed for the relief of pain. And, quite simply, he was mistaken!

July 24 • Friday • early morning

Mr. Breclaw called two more witnesses to testify about state regulations governing the sale of prescription drugs. The most significant information came from Paul Germak, a pharmacist with Highland Pharmacy in Highland, Indiana.

Mr. Germak was a member of the Indiana State Board of Inspection (Board of pharmacies). The board's function, among other things, was to oversee the proper dispensation of controlled substances (drugs) in accordance with state and federal regulations. The jury heard that reports concerning Dr. Koo's excessive writing of prescriptions for Valium and codeine for an unusually large number of patients over a long period of time were superficially investigated and then ignored.

It didn't take much effort for the jury to figure out that Tammy as well as many others on welfare were paying nothing for such treatment. Could it be that Dr. Koo and other doctors who treated a high percentage of welfare patients were milking the system? Did they do so to create patient dependency?

Mr. Breclaw called as his next witness for the defense Ms. Tammy Spasske Garza.

To support his sexual fantasy theory, he wanted to convince the jury that Tammy was taking far more medication than Dr. Koo had ever prescribed. He wanted to show that she was able to get refills and additional prescriptions filled at three pharmacies because substance control enforcement was ineffective at best — nonexistent at worst.

He also needed to establish a source for acid phosphatase other than his client. To do that he needed to convince the jury that Tammy had been sexually active within 72 hours of her rape kit test.

Tammy stuck to her previous testimony that her consumption of Valium was one tablet per day, sometimes two. She took codeine every four hours for pain as needed. If there was no pain she did not take any codeine.

Mr. Breclaw pressed her about birth control pills and she said, "I already stated before that my periods had been messed up ever since my daughter was born 10 years ago, on and off. Sometimes I'm regular, sometimes I'm not. I had a D & C to try to clear it up, and I'm always on birth control pills. The estrogen level regulates my periods, estrogen or hormones, I'm not sure."

Eventually, Breclaw brought out the point that Tammy's sister, Becky, was receiving similar medication from Dr. Koo, and was actually a patient of his right up until the start of the trial. He also got Tammy to testify that Becky lived in the garage apartment adjacent to where Tammy lived with her parents. As such Becky had access to Tammy's room and any medication that might have been there. In Tammy's own words, "I was never out of Valium, no, I always had it lying around. There was always tons of it. He always refilled it."

There was a huge quantity of Valium over and above what Tammy said she took. But Tammy explained once again, "I took one a day, two sometimes. This is just — if I took that much I'd be dead.''

Mr. Breclaw then zeroed in on Tammy's social life. He went after the details of her sexual relations with her boyfriend and when they ended. Tammy mentioned breaking up with him six weeks before March 30. She also testified as to not having sex with anyone for a month before March 30.

The two week gap seemed to bother counsel for the defense. He tried, by his questioning, to infer that since Tammy was on birth control pills she was having sex with someone else and may have had sex within the 72-hour window before March 30.

He took his own sweet time to do this and eventually exhausted the patience of the judge. Outside the hearing of the jury Judge Page asked, ''Mr. Breclaw, I'll reiterate that I am hesitant to cut you off from your examination of the complaining witness, but what is the point of all this?''

Mr. Breclaw answered, ''The point is, if she's having sex, she's with someone, that this would possibly be the reason for the acid phosphatase. She's taking birth control pills. Some women take it to control their periods, some don't, but she's answered that question.''

The judge responded with the obvious, ''My point is that we have been on this for nearly 55 minutes, and it would seem to me that that could have been answered in a simple — 'Were you taking birth control pills, and when was the last time you had sex prior to March 30, 1989?' ''

Unable to shake Tammy, the defense turned her over to Mr. Benson for cross-examination. He had her repeat her previous testimony that the last time she had sex before March 30 was at least a month prior. And he asked a few questions about Medicaid.

* * *

Q. "Are you aware of anyone else in your house who is taking Valium and codeine?"

A. "My sister."

Q. "Now, when you went in there for these prescriptions, you were on Medicaid at the time, correct?"

A. "Yes, sir."

Q. "What did you have to do in order to get your prescriptions with Medicaid?"

A. "They just wanted to see it one time, you get a Medicaid card every month, and it's got your name on it. It was just my daughter and me. It's good for one month, so when you took it in, like on the first, if they saw it on the first, you didn't have to show it again for the rest of the month. They had the information on file."

Q. "And were there ever occasions where that card was either lost by yourself or you put it somewhere and it wasn't there when you went back for it?"

A. "A couple times I had to call my caseworker and get it replaced because it just disappeared."

Q. "Was your sister residing in the house with you and your parents?"

A. "It was the house, but it was like adjoining garage. She could get into our side of the house any time she wanted."

* * *

For the rest of Friday, and for most of the following Monday, we heard from the obligatory character witnesses — patients and employees of Dr. Koo who expressed their respect and admiration for him.

July 27 • Monday • mid afternoon

Counsel for the defense then put Detective Sergeant Hedinger on the stand to testify about various police reports. From this witness we learned that the initial police investigation of Tammy's accusation of rape, before Sgt. Hedinger became involved, was sloppy. There was no attempt at a professional "crime scene" investigation until several days after the incident. By then Dr. Koo had had the opportunity to clean up his office. Even then the investigating officers didn't get any pictures and thus left open the questions about the sliding doors, examining tables, and lamps.

The judge then announced to the jury that their presence on Tuesday would not be required. He explained that the court had some legal matters to complete that did not involve the jury. He told us to enjoy our day off and to return bright and early Wednesday morning to get back to work.

We left the courtroom that evening with the realization that in the very near future we would begin deliberations to determine if Tammy's testimony was fact or fantasy. We might even determine the same of Dr. Sabelli's. But we never, in our wildest thoughts, envisioned the thunderbolt that would strike us Wednesday morning.

7

Suffer Little Children

July 29 • Wednesday • 9:30 a.m.

An unreal atmosphere pervaded the courtroom as we listened to a former employee of Dr. Koo, a prosecution witness, testify about the doctor's office routine. None of the court personnel — judge, bailiffs, or the attorneys — seem to be paying attention to the testimony. Yet the courtroom is almost filled, a strange contrast to the few spectators of the past six days. When the witness finished Judge Page began a long, detailed instruction to the jury. He emphasized the following.

* * *

THE COURT

The State has presented evidence to you from the complaining witness, Tammy Spasske, as to what took place on March 30, 1989. It is utmost and foremost your responsibility to determine whether or not, based on the evidence that's been presented to you, the State has established beyond a reasonable doubt that on March 30, 1989, Young Soo Koo had sexual intercourse with Tammy Spasske at a time when she was not aware that sexual intercourse was occurring.

Now, you have also heard extensive evidence on the subject of the drugs Valium and codeine and the possibility of them causing hallucinations and what have been identified to you as sexual fantasies.

The State now wishes to introduce evidence to you regarding two other patients. I will permit this evidence to come in for your consideration, but it is important that you only use it for the limited purpose for which I am permitting it in. I do not want you at any time to forget that the ultimate question here is whether or not what Tammy Spasske says took place on March 30, 1989, has been established beyond a reasonable doubt.

With these two witnesses that you will hear, you must, as with all witnesses, determine whether or not you believe what they have to say. If you determine that you believe what they have to say, you must then determine how what they have to say relates to the case at hand.

The State has indicated that they wish to bring this evidence forward as evidence that what Tammy Spasske says she saw on March 30, 1989, was not a hallucination. This evidence may be considered by you only for that purpose. It may be, and once again I say this is your decision alone, that you believe these other two witnesses and what they say to you, and for that reason it may be that you conclude that improprieties may have occurred on another date with other patients, but it is essential that you not in any way, because you believe these two people, convict Young Soo Koo of the charges against him just because you believe those two other people.

These other incidents are only being permitted to be brought forward for you to hear so that it may help you in determining whether or not you should believe Tammy Spasske.

* * *

She gave her name as Martha Mason and her age at the time of the trial as 22. Although her manner and her speech pattern were those of a mentally-retarded person, she had managed to finish most of her high school education. It was obvious she was not looking forward to testifying, but it was also obvious she was determined to do so anyway. Also, by her own admission, she was considerably overweight.

She had first gone to Dr. Koo in 1980 or 1981. For years she had problems with her stomach and her thyroid, but it was for an ear infection that her mother took her to see the doctor in January 1983. She was 12 years old.

A few minutes into her testimony Mr. Breclaw asked that Mr. Benson lead the witness. He gave as his reason his concern that she might inadvertently testify to things not asked. Rather then have this emotional young woman tell her story in her own words, he wanted her reduced to giving simple yes or no answers.

This technique should have softened the tone of her testimony. It would not, and did not, soften its impact. At every critical juncture Mr. Benson would ask her what happened next, and the jury got the story in the emotionally charged words of the witness herself.

Looking at the diagram of the doctor's office she identified room number two as where she was examined. Its doors, she said, were sliding. It was after her ears were examined that it began. "We were getting ready to leave," Martha said, "and I had asked him if there was any way I could get some diet pills because I was heavy then, well, still heavy, but he told me no, and then my mom started talking to him. Then he looked at my mom and said he was going to do a hormone smear, and he told her to leave the room. So my mom went out of the room, and he told me to get undressed, take my pants and panties off, So I did, and he watched me take them off, and then I got up on the table, the examining table, and he had pulled the step out that was attached to the table. Then he taped a piece of paper to the light.

"I put my feet in the stirrups. Alls I could see was the top of the doctor's head when he told me he was going to start the test.

"When he first started, it hurt real bad, and I pushed up on the table, and he took both of his hands and placed his hands, one on my right knee and pulled me down, and one on my left knee and pulled me down, and it hurt worse when he pulled me down. I did that — I pushed up about three or four times, and he would always pull me down.

"After the first time he pulled me down I got scared and started yelling 'I want my mom,' and he would start shaking.

"His hands — the whole time I was on the table he kept one hand on my right knee, and when I kept yelling I wanted my mother, his hands would like tremble, shake.

"He went out of the room once, and then he came back in, and then he supposedly started doing the test again, and then I got even louder, and my mom heard, I guess, because she knocked on the door, and he went out of the room again, came back in, and went over to the table, and I heard a zipper, and I don't know if it was zipping up or zipping down. Alls I heard was a zipper, and then my mom opened the door, and he motioned her in, and she came in, and we were sitting there.

"I asked Dr. Koo if I could go use the bathroom. I went in and when I wiped myself, at the time I didn't know, but when I wiped myself, the tissue was all full of snot.

"I had never seen semen before. Today I know that it looked like semen.

"I went back to the room and I told my mom I wanted to leave, and we went out to the truck, and I couldn't sit down — my bottom hurt real bad.

"We went home, and my mom called my aunt, and then my mom called the hospital, and that's when Mr. Hedinger and a couple of other people met me and my mom at the hospital.

"The nurse that was examining me had an instrument and she asked if Dr. Koo had used an instrument like that to do the hormone smear, and I said no. She asked me if Dr. Koo had any gloves on, and I said no.

"Then she used the instrument and took a smear. It was different than with Dr. Koo. The instrument was cold, and it only hurt for a few minutes. It pinched, and at the doctor's office nothing hurt like that. There it was warm, and it just kept hurting.

"The nurse took off her pair of gloves and asked me if that was the same sound I heard, and it wasn't. I heard a zipper and the zipper sound was different from the glove sound when the nurse took them off.

"I didn't know it then, but today I believe he raped me."

* * *

A sensitive defense attorney would have kept his cross-examination brief, no more than two or three minutes. The name of the game was to get this witness away from the jury as quickly as possible and not let her repeat her story a second time. Mr. Breclaw chose a different tactic. I never thought it possible for a mildly retarded witness to get the best of an attorney in a court of law. But a grand jury had failed to believe her story in 1983 and this was her second chance. Ms. Mason was clearly motivated to be a credible witness this time. It soon became a battle of wits against an unarmed opponent.

At the time she didn't know how effective her testimony would be. Each answer to each question was surrounded by a moat of sobs and a veil of tears. She struggled to hold herself together and just managed to do so. Salient portions of the three-hour cross-examination are as follows.

* * *

Q.   "And at that time they did what is called a rape kit on you, did they not?"

A.   "I don't know what it was called."

Q.   "Well, did they not take specimens of inside your vagina that they used for analysis?"

A.   "Yes."

Q.   "Now, the fact of the matter is that you don't know what that white substance was that you wiped from your vagina in January 1983, do you?"

A.   "I know what it looks like, and I know what it smells like now. It was the same thing."

Q.   "Do you remember appearing in a grand jury in this courtroom on March 16, 1983, about two months after this alleged incident in January 1983?"

A.   "Yes."

Q.   "In that grand jury did you not testify that you did not know what that particular white fluid was?"

A.   "No, I said it looked like snot."

Q.   "Now, you have a child, do you not?"

A.   "Yes."

Q.   "Before January 1983 did you have sexual intercourse with a male?"

A.   "No."

Q.   "When is the first time that you had sexual intercourse with a male?"

A.   "About four years ago."

Q.   "And how old were you at that time?"

A.   "Going on 18."

Q.   "Was that time the first time you had seen semen?"

A.   "Yes."

Q.   "So approximately five years elapsed between the time you looked at the white substance that was on your toilet paper in the washroom until the time that you first saw semen?"

A. "Yes."

Q. "And it's on the basis of seeing semen on that first time and possibly other times after that that you now draw the conclusion that what you saw you feel or believe was semen?"

A. "Yes, I do."

Q. "Now, on this day in question you did not see the doctor's penis, did you?"

A. "No."

Q. "Did doctor administer a shot, an injection into your arm?"

A. "No."

Q. "Throughout this whole procedure that you testified to, was Dr. Koo's wife in his medical office on Kennedy Avenue?"

A. "Yes, and I think one nurse was there."

Q. "You indicated that you were overweight at the time?"

A. "Yeah."

Q. "Do you recall how much you did weigh?"

A. "No, I know I was fat."

Q. "Since that time have you had other pelvic exams?"

A. "Yes, about six."

Q. "And were these all from the same physician, other than Doctor Koo?"

A. "They were all done by a female doctor, the same person."

Q. "And some of these had to do with the birth of your child?"

A.   "Yes."

Q.   "Now, you took your underwear off and got on the exam table. Did he give you a cloth to wrap around yourself?"

A.   "No, he just told me to put my feet in the stirrups."

Q.   "Did he give you a cloth prior to you scooting into the stirrups?"

A.   "No, he put — well, he put one on the table just like on my waist and taped it to the light."

Q.   "You stated he pulled a step out from the table. Did he stand on that table?"

A.   "Yes."

Q.   "Do you know how long he was on the step?"

A.   "Probably during the whole examination."

Q.   "But you really don't know, do you?"

A.   "No, but I do know that when he gets off the step you can't see him and I could see the top of his head from the top of the paper."

Q.   "Was it the corner of the drape or the middle of the drape that was taped to the light?"

A.   "It was the corner because the paper went like that" [indicating].

Q.   "Now, the paper extended down to your belly button, the other corner?"

A.   "Yes."

Q.   "Was the paper also sort of touching your knees?"

A.   "I don't think so."

                              *   *   *

A series of questions followed concerning the exact position of the light and Martha's knees. Mr. Breclaw was unable to get the specific answers he wanted and Martha became distraught. So much so that Judge Page tried to calm her by saying, "Mr. Breclaw is trying to get some details from you. Don't let it upset you."

* * *

Q. "Did you have any apprehension about taking off your clothes and then lying on a table?"

A. "I was kind of nervous, yes."

Q. "What was going through your mind?"

A. "I wanted my mom in the room with me."

Q. "Has your female physician ever inserted a speculum inside of you?"

A. "Yes."

Q. "Has she used her hands inside you before?"

A. "Yes."

Q. "Did you feel Dr. Koo touch your vagina with his hand?"

A. "I can't recall."

Q. "In other words, your testimony is that he may have touched your vagina with his hand?"

A. "I didn't say that. I just said I can't recall."

Q. "Do you recall whether or not Doctor put K-Y jelly onto your vagina?"

A. "No, he did not. Can I go?" [Witness very distraught.]

THE COURT

"Sure. You can't go completely, but do you want to take a break for a few minutes?"

THE WITNESS

"Yeah."

(A BRIEF RECESS IS TAKEN)

MR. BRECLAW

Q.   "Prior to going to the bathroom, did Doctor clean up your vaginal area with a gauze or any type of rubbing compound?"

A.   "No."

Q.   "And Doctor didn't touch you at all between the time your mother came in and the time you left for the washroom?"

A.   "No."

Q.   "At that time you didn't know what a penis felt like inside of your vagina, did you?"

A.   "No."

Q.   "And it was only some years later that in fact you had sexual intercourse?"

A.   "Yes."

Q.   "While you were lying there on the table, the drape prevented you from seeing what was being done?"

A.   "Yep."

Q.   "So therefore you don't know whether or not Dr. Koo put rubber gloves on?"

A.   "No, but he didn't have any on because when he pulled me down, you could feel his skin of his hand on my legs."

Q.   "Were you hysterical at that point?"

A.   "Yes, because I wanted to go home. I didn't want to be there."

Q.   "In your vaginal area, on your buttocks, thighs, the V in your crotch area, could you feel anything pressing against there?"

A.   "I felt cloth."

* * *

Mr. Breclaw then pointed out that Martha's answer to that question at the grand jury was, "No." Martha then said she did not remember the question or the answer. Mr. Breclaw pressed the point and Martha shot him down with her answer, "I was 13 years old then."

* * *

Q.   "Did Dr. Koo ejaculate inside of you?" [Long pause.]

THE COURT

"Is it the word?"

THE WITNESS

A.   "Uh-huh."

THE COURT

"Do you know what it means?"

THE WITNESS

A.   "Yeah, I know what it means."

THE COURT

"Are you able to answer the question?"

THE WITNESS

A.   "I don't know if he did or not. Alls I know is I found what today is called sperm when I went to the bathroom."

MR. BRECLAW

Q.   "At the time you testified in front of the grand jury you
      knew about the birds and the bees, did you not?"

A.   "I didn't know about it until after what happened. My
      mother told me when I was in the hospital laying on the
      bed."

                              * * *

Somewhat earlier in his cross-examination Mr. Breclaw had
covered the area of Martha calling for her mother. He asked a long
series of questions without surfacing anything the jury had not already heard in direct examination. He now returned to that area to
the dismay of everyone in the courtroom. Martha's answers to his
repeated questions became a mixture of sobbing, yelling, and crying. Toward the end it went as follows.

                              * * *

Q.   "What did you say, in your exact words? Did you say,
      'Mom, I want you. Mom, come in here?' "

A.   "No. I said, 'I want my mom.' "

Q.   "Tell me how loud was it. Were you hollering it?

A.   "I said, [screaming from the witness box], 'I want my
      mom.' That's loud enough for her to hear me."

Q.   "But yet on the other two to three occasions you were
      hollering this, Dr. Koo did not turn his back and go to the
      wall?"

A.   "Dr. Koo started shaking after I started yelling I wanted
      my mom. He walked out of the room twice."

Q.   "When was the first time that he walked out of the room,
      before your mom was there?"

A.   "Yes, the second time I said I wanted my mom he left me
      alone and walked out of the room and then came back."

Q.   "You yelled for your mother, he walked out of the room, and then you yelled for your mother again?"

A.   "No. I yelled for my mom, he started shaking. I yelled for her again, he walked out of the room, went into a different room, my mother said, and then he came back into the room where I was at."

Q.   "That's the first time you yelled for your mom?"

A.   "The second time I yelled for my mom."

Q.   "All right. The first time you yelled for your mom he didn't do anything?"

A.   "He started shaking."

Q.   "When was the third time you yelled for your mom?"

A.   "When he came back in the room and tried to do the test again."

Q.   "Now, what type of test was he trying to do?"

A.   "Supposedly he was going to do a hormone smear test, but that wasn't it because I know what an instrument feels like, and he did not have an instrument."

Q.   "Don't you think it's strange for the doctor to be raping you while you're hollering for your mother, when your mother is in the office and his wife is in the office?"

A.   "Yes, it's strange." [With that the court broke for lunch.]

Q.   "Now, in January 1983 was Doctor wearing his lab coat, his white lab coat?"

A.   "Yes."

Q.   "And was the lab coat open or was it buttoned?"

A.   "It was buttoned at the top but open down at the bottom."

Q.   "So it was unbuttoned from the waist down?"

A.   "Yes."

Q.   "When you called for your mom for the last time, did he state to you, 'The test is done.' "

A.   "Yes."

Q.   "When testifying in front of the grand jury do you remember being asked the question, His private and her private, I want to ask you what do you think Dr. Koo did to you on the examination table? Did he put something inside your private? Answer, yes. Question, what do you think this something was?

"Answer, what my mom said. Question, not what your mom said, what did you think it was? No response. Do you believe he put his private inside your private? I think. Why do you think so? Because he didn't have no instrument. Do you remember being asked those questions and giving those answers?"

A.   "Yeah, but like I said before, I was 13 when that was taken, and I was 12 when it happened."

* * *

Mr. Breclaw then concluded his cross-examination. Since Mr. Benson had no redirect, a sobbing Martha left the room. Before the jury could catch its breath another young woman took the stand. In appearance she was much like Martha. She was by no means retarded, but neither had she been in the top of her high school class.

Susan Long was born on October 14, 1968 and had been going to Dr. Koo, her family's doctor, since she was 12. In November, 1984, at the age of 16, she experienced flu-like symptoms and her mother called Koo's office for an appointment. The doctor indicated his schedule was filled but he would get back to her as soon as he was free. Susan then told the jury in her own words what transpired.

"Late that evening, when my mom was at work, about 7:30 or 8:00, he came to my house and picked me up and told me my mother said I needed to go to the office so that he could give me some medicine to make me better. I went with him to his office on Kennedy Avenue. The lights were off and no one else was there.

"I went into the second exam room and stood there. He put on a lab coat, a white coat with pockets in the front, and he stood at the door and he asked me to undress. I took off my pants, but I didn't take off my underclothing or my socks. He told me to sit on the table and he gave me a shot in my right arm, in the vein.

"I was laying there and I felt — I wasn't sleepy, but I felt like I was going to sleep or my body was going to sleep, but my mind wasn't, and he had a white cloth that he laid across me. He put my legs in the stirrups and taped my legs to the stirrups. Then he taped the cloth to the light, and I couldn't see anything but the top of his head from about this point on. I got real scared, and then he said, 'Now I told you to take off your clothes,' and he had to take the tape off one leg to get my underwear off, and then he taped my leg back up.

"He turned his back towards me, and the only reason I can say that was because I could just see the back of his head, and I can remember hearing his buckle unbuckle and his zipper, and at that point he turned back to me, and I could feel him touching my legs and pulling me to the end of the table, and I just didn't believe that. I was crying and trying to lift up the cloth so I could see what he was doing, and he yelled at me and told me to stop and lie still, and he put his hand so that I couldn't move the blanket, and then he just kind — I could see him moving and I could feel his hands touching me and touching my stomach and my legs, touching me and rubbing me.

"I could feel him moving back and forth inside me. It seemed like forever, but I'm sure it was only maybe 10 minutes, if that. It just — but it just seemed like it was forever.

"I had these exams before but this was different. Before, I would be talked through it and explained, you know, this was going to feel cold, of this was going to hurt a bit, and what was one of the strangest parts was I felt really comfortable because of the way he talked to me, even though I couldn't see anything.

"But this time his voice changed and he was real — he kind of yelled at me. He had never done that before, he was always real nice to me, and like I said, he always told me before what he was doing. And before what I felt inside me was cold. Now what I felt inside me was warm, not cold like the speculum. Then he stopped and grabbed a paper towel. I could hear what sounded like latex or rubber, like someone was removing rubber gloves, but he didn't have gloves on because I could feel his hands when he touched me, and he turned the faucet on for a second and turned it back off, and he had a garbage can that had a peddle on it, so when you would let go of the peddle, the garbage can would make a popping sound, and I heard him put something — wrap something up in the paper towel or crumble the paper towel up, and he threw it in the garbage and took his foot off and the garbage can shut, and he walked to the side of me, told me to get up and get dressed, and I laid there because I was still feeling real sick, and I was kind of scared, and I felt like I was dozing off to a point, but yet it wasn't like a steady sleep, it wasn't like I was going to sleep. He walked out of the room and a few moments later he came back and told me it was time to go and I needed to get dressed. So I got up and I put my underpants back on and my pants and I didn't put my socks on. I told him I was kind of tired and I didn't feel real good, and he just said, 'Hurry up, it's time to go,' and we left the office.

"Then he asked me if I was hungry, and I said no, I felt sick and I wanted to go home. He stopped on the way at McDonald's and bought me food anyway, and I still wasn't hungry.

"He told me, he said, 'You were a good girl,' and then he didn't really say a whole lot, other than that. He asked me what I wanted and I said I didn't want anything, and he took me back to my mother's and walked me in to the front apartment door. He walked inside to where my brother and my cousin Jeff were, and he asked them if they wanted the food because I wasn't hungry, and they sat down on the couch to eat it.

"I didn't see my mother till the next afternoon. I told her that he came to pick me up and took me to his office because I was sick, and she kind of got a little upset about it, and she sat there for a second, and I told her that I felt like he touched me and made me feel funny. I was too embarrassed to say anything else.

"My mother said that what had happened — when I told her I felt uncomfortable, she said that a lot of times when you have a pelvic exam that you do, and I just tried to accept it because of my mother. I was so embarrassed to say anything to my mother like that, like I was supposed to, because I didn't want anyone to be mad at me.

"She had me keep on seeing him until I was 18. And then he started giving me money. November 1985, was the first time. I had gotten out of the hospital that day and wanted to go to turnabout (a high school dance where the girls ask the boys and pay for everything). He knew my mother didn't have very much money because she had recently been divorced, so he told me that if I took good care of myself, that he would release me from the hospital, and he gave me three hundred dollars to buy myself a dress or some clothes or something nice to wear. He told me I was a good girl and that he wanted me to have nice things.

"For my wedding he sent me a three hundred dollar check. That was October 18 of '86, four days after my eighteenth birthday.

"Then in 1990 I was seeing a counselor and telling him what exactly had happened and how it made me feel, and he said I needed to talk to my mother and let her know. A couple weeks later I broke down and told her and she said she was going to go to the office and confront him and talk to him.

"Her and I both went because she wanted me to be there. They put us in the examining room and Dr. Koo walked in and he said,

'Well, how are you?' And my mom said, 'Not very good,' and I started crying and I stood up and I walked out because I just couldn't stand to be near him.

"The next day his nurse called my mother's home and said that there was something there for up to pick up, and my mother told me to go by and pick it up. It was a check for $400 and on the bottom left-hand corner was written 'refund.' That was funny because we never paid him anything."

It was brought out during cross-examination that Dr. Koo billed Susan's mother's ex-husband's insurance company for 70 percent of the bill. The other 30 percent was to have been billed directly to Susan's mother but was never so billed. Dr. Koo never billed any medical service to either Susan or her mother.

Mr. Benson finished his direct examination by asking Susan what she now believed the doctor did to her on that evening in November 1984. Susan testified that she had no doubt at all that Dr. Koo raped her.

* * *

Just minutes into the cross-examination by Mr. Breclaw the court with all its constituents — bailiffs, court reporter, judge, jury, attorneys, newspaper reporters, and spectators — became unwilling witnesses to testimony so powerful that many were openly crying. Susan's answers were spaced between periods of sobbing and choking back her tears.

We learned that Susan had given her statement to Detective Sergeant Hedinger on January 24, 1991, but had never reported her allegations of rape to the police prior to that date.

Knowing that Susan had continued to visit Dr. Koo for medical treatments until she was 18, counsel for the defense wanted to develop the point that someone who believed they had been raped was not likely to return over and over to the doctor she believed had raped her. He thought he could damage her credibility by asking her about those return visits.

* * *

Q. "Now, between November of 1984 and June of 1990, did you continue to receive medical treatment at Dr. Koo's office?"

A. "I no longer received medical attention after I was 18, and I no longer had to go to him because I was a minor."

Q. "Prior to 1984 Dr. Koo had not made any suggestive comments to you, had he?"

A. "On one other occasion I felt really uncomfortable when he listened to my heart."

Q. "Well, in other words, he was — tell me a little about that. When was that occasion?"

A. "Probably a few months earlier."

Q. "Did he have a stethoscope?"

A. "Yes, he did."

Q. "And did he put that inside your blouse?"

A. "He put it under my blouse."

Q. "And he was listening to your heart?"

A. "What he says to be my heart."

Q. "And was it on your breast?"

A. "Yes, it was."

Q. "And what else happened?"

A. "I just felt as if he fondled me."

Q. "What do you mean by that?"

A. "Just the way he held my breast."

Q. "How did he hold your breast?"

A.   "He just kind of squeezed it and put his hand over it with the stethoscope between his fingers."

Q.   "And you interpret this as possibly him being fresh with you?"

A.   "Now I wouldn't say that. Then I just felt uncomfortable. I was a little girl, and I felt uncomfortable."

Q.   "But now in your mind do you think that he was doing that to arouse his sexual desires?"

A.   "I'm unable to answer a question that only he could."

Q.   "So what you're telling this jury is that you wait six years after this incident to confront Dr. Koo about raping you?"

A.   "I was very ashamed, so yes."

Q.   "After 1984 how many pelvic examinations did you have in Dr. Koo's office?"

A.   "What he called pelvic examinations, probably six."

Q.   "During these other pelvic examinations would Dr. Koo tape your feet into the stirrups?"

A.   "Yes, he would ask my mother to leave, he would inject me with a shot, he would tape my legs — "

Q.   "Let me ask the question. You say he would ask your mother to leave?"

A.   "Yes."

Q.   "In 1985 was your mother present in Dr. Koo's examining room when Dr. Koo taped your ankles into the stirrups?"

A.   "Yes."

Q.   "In 1985 was your mother present in the examining room when Dr. Koo gave you a shot intravenously into your arm prior to a pelvic examination?"

A. "Yes."

Q. "In 1985 was your mother present in the examining room when Dr. Koo took the sheet and taped it to the goose-neck lamp?"

A. "Yes, she was."

Q. "In fact, she was present on all other occasions, was she not?"

A. "No, she was not. I can think of two other occasions where she left the room, and he did not only tape my feet, but he taped my legs to the side."

Q. "You had a sheet around your waist, did you not?"

A. "From about midway down."

Q. "And you were undressed below the sheet, you were na-ked?"

A. "Yes."

Q. "So about half of the pelvic examinations you received after November of 1984 your mother was present in the room while you were being taped to the stirrups and also while you were administered the shot, an intravenous shot?"

A. "Yes, she was."

Q. "And you permitted this procedure to take place with your mother in the room even though in your own mind you knew that Dr. Koo had raped you in the same manner in November of 1984?"

A. "I was very — "

Q. "Just yes or no, please."

A. "Yes."

Q. "And did you not tell your mother about Dr. Koo raping you — look at me, please."

MR. BENSON

> "I object. She doesn't have to look at Mr. Breclaw. If she's disgusted by the question, she does not have to look at him. She doesn't have to look at his client or anyone else."

MR. BRECLAW

Q.   "You did not tell your mother about Dr. Koo raping you until a few weeks before June of 1990."

A.   "Yes."

Q.   "Do you know whether or not the four hundred dollars was given to you for purposes of paying for counseling for emotional problems."

A.   "I cannot say why he gave me the check, but I do know that he wrote refund there, and I was not due a refund because I had never paid him."

Q.   "I understand that that was given to you out of whatever, generosity of his heart possibly. The question is — "

MR. BENSON

"I object, Your Honor, and move to strike that comment by defense counsel."

THE COURT

"Let's move along, gentlemen. The jury can sort the wheat from the chaff."

MR. BRECLAW

Q.   "Would it not be true that for several years you have been a very emotionally-disturbed young lady?"

A. "After this incident I had a lot of problems dealing with it because I kept it locked up inside of me, and it bothered me very bad."

Q. "You had no problem with accepting the money Dr. Koo was giving you, especially the three hundred dollars initially, did you?"

A. "I just never said anything. I just didn't want anyone to be mad at me, and I didn't want to be embarrassed, and I didn't want anyone to know."

Q. "Ms. Long, would it be your testimony that in fact every time that you went into Dr. Koo's office during which he taped your ankles to the stirrups that he had sexual intercourse with you?"

A. "Yes, I do believe what he called a pelvic examination was in fact rape."

Q. "How many times after 1984 did Dr. Koo have sexual intercourse with you?"

A. "I can't say for sure. I can say I had approximately seven pelvic examinations with that one included, the first one, and I can't give an exact answer."

Q. "Each of these times your feet were taped into the stirrups?"

A. "Yes."

Q. "Each of these times you had a shot in your arm?"

A. "Yes."

Q. "No exceptions?"

A. "No."

Q. "Did you ever make a complaint to a police department?"

A. "No."

Q.   "Did you ever make a complaint to the doctor's assistants?"

A.   "No."

Q.   "Is one of the reasons you didn't bring it up because you wanted to continue receipt of the money?"

A.   "No, it was not."

Q.   "Ms. Long, is this whole episode by any chance just a figment of your imagination?"

A.   "No, it is not."

Q.   "You continue to voluntarily go to him for medical treatment for several years after 1984?"

A.   "I was under 18, he was my family physician, and my mother told me to so I did what I was told."

Q.   "Even after 18 you continued to go to him?"

A.   "No, I did not."

Q.   "Didn't you, for example, when you got blood work for your wedding, didn't you go to him?"

A.   "It was four days prior to my eighteenth. I did ask to go to someone different, but my mother had sent him a wedding invitation, and she talked to him on the phone, and he said part of a gift to me was to give me my blood work and to my husband because we did not have very much money and I was marrying — my husband had been injured prior to this and wasn't working, so he did not have any money, and he wanted to give us something, and I still didn't feel comfortable with Dr. Koo."

Q.   "Why couldn't you have gone with your own money and got another doctor to get you a blood test?"

A.   "Just days after my wedding I had not been feeling well, and I did in fact see a doctor of my own."

Q.   "What I'm saying is when you're engaged to be married, four days before the wedding, you're employed, you have money, you're ashamed of what this doctor did to you, you're emotionally sick about what he did to you, your mother and your family has money, they're receiving child support, you have a dislike for this doctor, can you give me an explanation of why you just didn't take a little bit of money and go to another doctor for a blood test, a simple blood test?"

A.   "Because it was supposed to be a gift and I tried — I tried to make myself forget it happened, and I just figured one more time is all I had to go back, and it was only a blood test and there were going to be people in the room so I didn't have to worry about anything, and I'd never have to see him again."

Q.   "In fact, Ms. Long, it never did happen, did it?"

A.   "Yes, it did happen."

Q.   "The reason you went back was because it never happened?"

A.   "No, it did happen."

Q.   "Didn't you accept his gift of a free blood test as part of a wedding present to you?"

A.   "I told you what I did."

Q.   "And didn't you accept his money that he sent you in a card for your wedding?"

A.   "Yes, I did."

* * *

The only point Mr. Breclaw made in his favor was when Susan recalled the doors as swinging. Mr. Benson put a merciful end to her testimony with three questions on redirect.

* * *

Q.   "Susan, these times when your mother was present when he taped your legs and gave you an injection for a pelvic examination, what did Dr. Koo always do before he started the exam."

A.   "Always asked my mother to leave the room."

Q.   "And did she?"

A.   "Yes, he told her that it was best because I would be much easier to deal with and be calm."

Q.   "And did you want your mother to stay?"

A.   "Yes, I did. I asked her all the time."

* * *

8
Between Two Worlds

July 30 • Thursday • early morning

The last witness having testified, Judge Page provided the jury with the answer to one of the questions raised during the trial. The bailiffs produced a VCR so the jury could view a 17-minute video used by doctors to demonstrate the correct procedure for conducting a pelvic examination. It was a nice balance to the "zipper" lesson so enjoyed by the women of the jury. By then we had become so jaded by all the intimate details that one more anatomy lesson did not cause any embarrassment at all.

The final arguments from both attorneys took five hours — an hour and a half for the prosecutor, three for the defense.

The defendant was never called to give sworn testimony. To do so would have subjected him to cross-examination by Mr. Benson, and Mr. Breclaw did not want that to happen.

The prosecution stressed that the testimony from Tammy, Martha, and Susan came from depositions or statements made at different times, independent of the others. He pointed out the similarities of the three allegations and suggested that it would have been too great a coincidence for three independent stories to match up in so many details. He thought it unlikely that three people would experience identical "fantasies."

He emphasized that, as a doctor, Koo was able to clean his victims to remove physical evidence. He noted the difficulties faced by rape victims, and asked for a verdict of guilty. The defense stressed the availability of unlimited drugs and argued that Tammy was not able to handle the large quantities she had obtained from various pharmacies. Under the influence of what he claimed was an overdose, she had imagined a sexual event that had not taken place.

He noted the long and trusting relationship Dr. Koo had with Tammy and her family and suggested that no doctor would put his practice at risk by such improper conduct. Dr. Koo's actions at every step were consistent with good medical practice. He said that intercourse could never have taken place without the paper drape being torn or at least moved around or rustled. Tammy's view of the doctor's penis, he observed, was brief and could very well have been a mistaken impression. A glimpse for a fleeting second was not enough to convict a doctor of such a serious crime. He said there was no physical evidence.

Martha, he said, was simply mistaken and noted that the rape kit test failed to yield any physical evidence of sexual activity. He noted that the grand jury decided not to bring charges against Dr. Koo.

Susan's story didn't make sense, he argued, because she accepted Dr. Koo's gifts and continued seeing him. He suggested her story was triggered by Tammy's story in the newspapers.

He noted that Dr. Koo did not testify because he couldn't express himself well in English. In the end he appealed to our common sense and reason and asked for a verdict of not guilty.

By then the courtroom was crowded with spectators. About 20 Koreans sat behind Dr. Koo, while similar groups clustered about Tammy, Martha, and Susan. The jury seemed caught between two different worlds. A lot of people would be devastated by our verdict, I thought. We'd better get it right.

The judge issued final instructions and we adjourned to the jury room. It wasn't until well after the trial that I figured out why I was elected foreman. As the oldest man on the panel, I was obviously the least sexually threatening.

I suggested that we go around the table for general comments before voting. We took that first vote at 5:45 p.m. — six votes for guilty; three not guilty; three abstaining.

Once more I went around the room asking for anyone who wished to explain the reason for their vote. I also asked that jurors feel free to bring up any specific point they wished discussed by the group. For the next two hours it was a mix of free-for-all discussion and fast-cooling pizza.

I didn't feel it would be appropriate for me to tell the other jurors about my technical reason for doubting the testimony of Dr. Sabelli. But I did ask for a discussion about the sexual fantasy and situationally-induced hallucination theory. As it turned out, there wasn't much of a discussion.

The fantasy theory never got off the ground in the jury room. In the opinion of all, the idea of such a fantasy was ludicrous. It was just too far out.

So was the whole thing about all the drugs. Hour after hour, day after day, we had been subjected to a mountain of pharmacy records that Mr. Breclaw claimed to prove that Tammy was abusing Valium and codeine — taking much, too much.

We had a real down-to-earth jury. We zeroed in on the key points — yes, Tammy was on Valium and codeine. They had been prescribed by Dr. Koo. After Tammy left Dr. Koo's office on March 30 she drove without incident to Walgreen's where the pharmacist testified she was alert and in control — upset to the point of hysteria, but certainly not spaced-out. Shortly thereafter she was examined by a nurse and a doctor who also testified to her sober condition. Her urine analysis showed medium to high levels of both drugs from whatever quantities she had ingested but further testimony showed that Tammy could very well have built up a tolerance to those levels.

So she was on drugs. Dr. Koo didn't think it necessary to have her wait in the office until the effects of the shot had worn off. He let her drive away. And we had the three fully-qualified witnesses who saw her that evening. It didn't look like drugs played any part at all in what Tammy saw or felt. There was general agreement that Tammy believed her story. There was no question that she was telling the truth as she saw it. There was, however, the real possibility that she was mistaken. We had not discarded that possibility because we had discarded the drug/fantasy theory that supported it.

It was a fine line. We thought there was a real chance that Tammy's quick sighting of the doctor's penis might have been a false sighting that triggered her thoughts about his other actions and led her to believe she was raped when she really wasn't. This was never thought to be the result of the drugs or any sort of hallucination. It might have been due to the ordinary, everyday event when any of us gets a quick look at something — out of the corner of an eye, so to speak — and mistakenly identifies it because our mind was elsewhere. This was an area of reasonable doubt that need to be resolved.

"The doors" question was also handled in a practical manner.

The testimony about sliding/swinging doors was conflicting, so we had no way of knowing the truth. The real question was did it make any difference which room Tammy was in. The only way that mattered was if Dr. Koo were concerned about his receptionist walking in and seeing him in the act. Since the doctor told Tammy's father he was trying to have an affair with his receptionist (Beverly) the jury didn't think it mattered to Dr. Koo one bit. Thus "the doors" went down the drain.

We took another vote at 6:30 p.m. — seven guilty, three not guilty, two abstaining. While in theory the ballots were secret, there was no special effort by anyone to be secretive. Some jurors indicated how they voted, others did not. No one asked how anyone voted; no one seemed to care. We were trying to sort it out in our minds — each in his or her own way.

The actual ballots were small squares of paper that could be folded before being picked up by the alternate juror. In the beginning all the papers were folded. Towards the end many were left open.

During dinner one of the women, Lora, voiced her opinion to the group that she didn't feel comfortable with people abstaining. She felt everyone should commit one way or another. She had the idea that some of us were waiting to see how everyone else was voting before we did so ourselves.

I guess it's all in how you look at it. I explained to her and to the entire jury that I had thus far abstained for two reasons. First, I didn't want to influence others so early in our deliberations. Second, I felt that Koo was probably guilty but had not as yet resolved all the areas of reasonable doubt. I didn't want to vote not guilty when I thought he was guilty, and I didn't want to vote guilty until I was sure.

I could, however, see her point. It was rather obvious that Lora thought the doctor was guilty and had voted accordingly. I announced that I would no longer abstain. I would vote not guilty until I had satisfied myself that reasonable doubt no longer existed. If and when that happened I would vote guilty. This fit the rationale that a defendant must be presumed innocent until such reasonable doubt is resolved against him.

The 7:10 p.m. vote was eight guilty, four not guilty.

The discussion then shifted to the actual act in question. In spite of all the testimony, we had a number of questions concerning the possibility of the act taking place between individuals positioned as they were. Back and forth we went. Some of the jurors, male and female, went into positional details that seemed to be taken from personal experience. It started to get a bit out of hand as some positional possibilities surfaced remarks like, "Sure you can do it like that!" and "Well, I never would even think of doing it like that." and "Once you get by the bone structure the angle doesn't make any difference. You just go in and then it doesn't matter." (That last comment was from a female.)

One question seemed difficult to resolve from our collective prior experience. There had been testimony that the paper drape never moved, rustled, or been torn or damaged. Was intercourse possible without something happening to the paper?

Since neither side had been able to provide us with any kind of demonstration it looked to me like we needed our own demo. I suggested the idea by announcing, "I hate to bring this up, but until we can resolve this area we're going to have trouble getting to a proper verdict. What I'd like to propose is that one of the women here volunteer to play the part of the victim and, for obvious reasons, another woman play the part of the doctor. We have a paper drape (one of the exhibits), we have a table (jury table), and we can reverse two chairs so that their backs may serve as stirrups. What do you guys think?"

To my surprise one of the women volunteered at once. It was Jan, the female alternate. Fortunately, she was the devil-may-care, fun-loving one in the group. More fortunately she was wearing a pair of blue jeans. Jan said it was her opportunity as an alternate to make a useful contribution to the jury.

We cleared a corner of the table, reversed two chairs, found someone's umbrella to serve as the lamp (one person on each side of the victim held the umbrella horizontally), unfolded the paper drape, and (with scotch tape) taped it to the umbrella.

The height of the jury table was about 27 inches. One of the doctors had testified that the exams tables were 36 inches high. The standard household step (as close as practical to the height of the pull-out step) being eight inches we figured we were within an inch or so of the distance between the top of the step and the top of the table. Our "doctor" would be at the right height if standing on the floor.

Jan got herself in place and our woman doctor stood up to walk over to her spot between Jan's legs. For most of the jury it was an emotional release, something to be taken lightly with a bit of the wink, wink — nudge, nudge type of humor. Even Jan seemed to be enjoying her center-stage role. But, under the surface, the tension was still there.

As the woman playing the doctor approached the corner of the table, one of the male jurors stood up and stepped back to allow her to pass. A startled Jan, thinking the man was going to move between her legs, drew back in fear saying, "Oh no, oh no!"

When the reason for his movements became obvious to Jan she slid herself down the table and put her feet back on the "stirrups." The devil-may-care attitude was gone.

We walked our actors through their parts several times, each time positioning the umbrella and paper drape differently. We eventually found the spot where the paper could be draped in such a way as to permit intercourse without being disturbed.

When the paper hung directly over the victim's navel it was far enough in from the end of the table to avoid contact with someone standing at the end of the table. The table acted as a barrier to prevent that person from touching the drape. We worked out the angle bit, the height bit, and the "hands on the legs" bit to satisfy ourselves that intercourse under the conditions of the testimony was not only possible, but relatively simple to effect.

As volunteer "stage hands" put everything back, Judge Page asked me to step into the hall. He wanted to know if we were likely to reach a verdict before 8:00 p.m., the cutoff time for hotel reservations for the jury. He also indicated that phones would be made available for any juror to call home for any clothing or toilet articles they might need at the hotel.

I promised a 7:45 p.m. ballot. Then he wanted to know if I thought the jury would be able to reach a unanimous verdict. I told him yes, but more time was needed for some of the jurors to be satisfied that all areas had been considered.

The 7:45 p.m. vote was unchanged — eight guilty, four not guilty. I reported it to the judge, made my phone call home, packed up my gear (thermos, chess set, note pad) and headed with the others to the parking lot. There under escort by the bailiffs we drove in convoy to a local hotel.

July 31 • Friday • 9:00 a.m.

When the jury reconvened I announced my intention to go through the major points before taking another vote. By so doing we would make sure we had touched all the bases and not overlooked any area of reasonable doubt. After a couple hours of debate the jury members eliminated everything except two critical areas on which we could now concentrate — the truth of Tammy's testimony and the source of the acid phosphatase on her underpants. During this process of elimination we requested a second viewing of the pelvic exam video in a manner that would allow us to stop the action at key points.

This was intended to supplement what we had learned during our own private demo about the positions and angles involved. We skipped the preliminaries and went to the cutaway diagram that showed the internal organs and movements of the doctor's fingers during the bimanual portion. We went through this part frame by frame. Our basic question was whether or not the patient could easily distinguish between the feeling of the fingers and the feeling of a penis.

It was not an easy thing for the men on the jury to decide and it took a woman's "touch" to get us straightened out. After a lengthy and unproductive discussion, an exasperated Lora rose to her feet and leaned forward over the jury table. She extended the two fingers and flicked them back and forth while explaining, "The fingers go in. They go to one side and then the other like this. Then they go out. It's not difficult at all to feel the difference."

The actions of Dr. Koo with Tammy's father were judged those of a guilty man rather than those of an innocent one. My personal feeling was if he were innocent, and as smart as a doctor is supposed to be, he would have called his receptionist into the office the minute Tammy got off the table. Then he would have called the police so that they could collect whatever evidence was applicable before sending Tammy to the hospital for the rape kit test. An innocent man would take strong and immediate steps to demonstrate his innocence, so I reasoned.

When I raised the point about a doctor's view of the female genitals not being sexually stimulating, it was Lora again who closed the subject by saying, "It is for a pervert like Koo!"

Some of the guys went into the men's room to test the zipper theories. Some of them did a demo in the presence of the women to demonstrate the sound of a zipper. Strange jury duty, this was.

We had as one of the exhibits a latex glove. We used it to compare the sound of removing the glove with the up and down sound of the zipper. The sounds were quite different. We then used a gloved hand and a bare hand to test a blindfolded juror's ability to distinguish between the two. It was no contest. The juror was able to detect the difference wherever he was touched on his bare skin.

Eventually it came down to two things — Tammy's word as she testified and the physical evidence of the acid phosphatase. It was never, as the public thought, a matter of her word against his. Dr. Koo had not testified and could not be cross-examined. His word could not be put to that test and was, in no way, to be considered as evidence. What we had was her unrefuted testimony under oath that withstood 16 hours of grueling cross-examination.

At that point there was just one woman who wasn't convinced that Tammy wasn't making some of this up. It took a round table discussion to eventually bring her around.

That left us with the only physical evidence that had any meaning at all — acid phosphatase on Tammy's underpants. We all agreed that the absence of additional physical evidence did not indicate innocence. That was to be expected in any case of rape by a doctor who had the opportunity to clean up traces of his body fluids. But where could the acid phosphatase have come from, if not Dr. Koo?

I suggested to the jury that we open the sealed rape kit to examine Tammy's underpants. Whenever the subject of women's panties comes up in mixed company it can get sticky. And, in this crowded jury room in Crown Point, it got very sticky.

Lora was adamant in her opposition. "What the hell do we need to look at that for," she yelled.

It was not a question; it was a statement. She paused for effect, then continued, "You get some kind of kick out of looking at women's underwear?"

That was a question and a statement.

The other women were on Lora's side. None of them would even consider looking at the panties, and they were not happy being in a room with a bunch of men who would.

I tried to explain that this was the only physical evidence we had, and we had better check it out against the possibility of the acid phosphatase having been present on the panties before Tammy showed up for her exam.

Lora was disgusted. Once again she asked what I expected to find. Rather than attempt some long explanation, I took the bull by the horns and replied, "Actually, I've got this panty fetish that I need to satisfy."

With that the room fell silent and I notified the bailiff that we would be breaking the seal on the rape kit to examine its contents. A few minutes later I did just that, assisted by two male jurors.

Predictably, when we finished, Lora asked, "Well, what good did that all do?"

This time I had a ready answer. "The pants were obviously clean. It's unlikely they had been worn for more than a few hours. The stain we heard about is so light that I couldn't see it. The location of the samples that tested positive for acid phosphatase are where you would expect had fluid from the vagina been its carrier. The dark streak was well away from the crotch area and could in no way be connected with fecal material or blood. There were no other markings or staining to indicate fecal material or blood. What I see is powerful evidence that Tammy wore clean underpants to the doctor's office and that the acid phosphatase could not have come from any source other than Dr. Koo. As far as I am concerned the acid phosphatase at those levels is physical evidence that Dr. Koo did engage in sexual intercourse with Tammy. Given Tammy's testimony that she was unaware of what was happening and certainly did not give her consent, I am convinced beyond reasonable doubt that Dr. Koo is guilty of rape," I replied.

With the foreman of the jury now openly on her side, Lora had no choice but to forgive and forget; well, maybe just forgive.

We went around the room once more and then, at 11:35 a.m., took a vote. The results were 11 for guilty, one not guilty.

"Let's break early for lunch," I suggested, "We don't need to identify our holdout just now."

But the holdout, another Korean War vet, spoke up, "I've got no objection. I'm the one who voted not guilty. I'm just not convinced he did it."

Okay," I answered, "I'm ready for lunch right now. It's been a long morning and I think we all need a break."

Outside the jury room the judge took me aside to ask how things were going. I told him I thought we should reach a verdict sometime that afternoon. He said he wanted to be informed when we did but did not want to know what the verdict was. It was his custom to remain in the dark until the verdict was read in court. Only then would the signed verdict slip be handed to the bailiff who would take it to the judge.

I was also informed that the courtroom would be sealed and extra police present to insure crowd control. Jurors would be dismissed first and given time to reach their cars and clear the parking lot before anyone else was released from the court.

During lunch I gave no thought at all about what would take place when we returned to the jury room to resume deliberations.

When we finally took our seats at the jury table I had nothing to say.

One awkward moment followed another until the holdout broke the silence. "I don't think there is any way I can change the minds of 11 of you, so I . . . ," he began.

That was when Lora came through. In a strong voice, charged with three weeks of pent-up emotion, she interrupted him in mid-sentence, "No! No! You can't do that. You can't change your vote just because of what the others think. We won't accept that. You've got to be convinced yourself. You've got to vote what you feel."

Her remarks were immediately echoed by the other women and most of the men. No one would accept a vote from anyone that did not vote their conscience.

So the hard-nosed Lora was fair after all, I thought. In her mind Koo was guilty, but she would never be satisfied with any verdict that was not the result of fair and impartial deliberation.

Now, what the hell do you do when you have a holdout in a rape case? I decided at once that it would not be wise to ask him why. That would only make him the target of deliberations yet to come. Hostility was something to be avoided at all cost.

I chose, instead, to review the major points — Tammy's testimony and the acid phosphatase. I told the jury that those were the key areas — everything else was secondary. I asked each juror to tell the group why they voted guilty — confining their reasons to Tammy's testimony and the acid phosphatase.

The vote at 1:45 p.m. was unchanged.

During a comfort break the holdout whispered to me that he was almost convinced, but needed a little more time. I asked him to let me know when he was ready for another vote.

At 2:20 p.m. I detected a slight nod in my direction and called for the final vote. I counted the ballots and announced the total to the jury — 12 guilty.

The bailiff was notified that we had reached our decision. He handed me the court verdict slips, one for guilty and one for not guilty, telling me to sign the appropriate slip, fold it, and return it to him after reading it in court.

July 31 • Friday • 3:00 p.m.

The jury returned to the jury box and the eerie silence of a packed courtroom. There I read the following:

We the jury find the defendant, Young Soo Koo, guilty of rape, a felony.

There was not a sound. My eye caught John Breclaw slump in his tracks, then reach over to grasp Dr. Koo by the shoulders in a gesture of disbelief and disappointment. On the other side of the room I saw smiles of joy on the faces of three extraordinary young ladies. Then it was back to work as Judge Page polled the jury to confirm our unanimity.

I barely remember our walk to the parking lot. There was no thought of getting together. Each and every juror simply wanted to leave. Five minutes later I awoke to find myself back in the real world, driving westward on Route 30 toward home.

Back in the courtroom a stunned Dr. Koo handed his car keys and wallet to a friend and reached over the railing to hug a few of the church women who had attended that day as a show of support from the Korean community. Handcuffed and under heavy guard, Dr. Koo was then escorted from the courtroom. Neither his wife nor his two children were present.

Close by, a sobbing Tammy was embracing her husband while tears of joy formed in the eyes of Martha and Susan. As they walked slowly from the courtroom to the hallway, Tammy hugged the two girls and told them, "Thank you, thank you for coming forward."

When she reached the hallway, Tammy lifted her head and announced to the world at large, "I hope he rots in hell. I've been dreaming about this ever since March 30, 1989. He raped me! He raped other women! He got what he deserves!"

Back in the courtroom, Phil Benson sat at the prosecutor's table, astounded by the verdict. He could hardly believe it. Not five minutes earlier he thought he had lost the case. Seeking some clue, any clue, he studied the jury as they returned to the courtroom. For a brief moment he thought he found one. For there, at the end of the line, was Lora, hard-nosed Lora, openly sobbing her heart out.

9
Victims on Parade

Bail for Dr. Koo was denied in an August 6, 1992 hearing. The Gary *Post-Tribune* quoted Judge Page as stating that the 51-year-old Hammond physician "was a danger to his patients and might flee the country if freed."

Mr. Benson was quoted in the same article as saying that "Koo violated orders from the Illinois Department of Professional Regulation to take a class on prescribing drugs. The Illinois regulatory agency fined Koo $1,500 and put him on probation for 12 months in September 1989, after discovering that Koo was prescribing drugs without a valid Illinois license."

Mr. Benson was quoted that, "according to two witnesses, Koo violated a 1991 temporary order from the Indiana Medical Licensing Board that he stop performing pelvic examinations that required a female to disrobe."

At a sentencing hearing in the State of Indiana both sides present witnesses before the judge — there is no jury. The normal rules of evidence don't apply. The judge is presumed to know what he should and should not consider. There is a direct examination and a cross-examination. The State tries to show why the guilty party should receive the maximum sentence, while the defense pleads for a lessor sentence. The plaintiff may testify, subject to cross-examination, and may also make a statement as to the harm she has suffered. The convicted party may also make a statement in his or her own behalf.

August 25 • Tuesday • 9:30 a.m.

T. Edward Page presided over the sentencing hearing where Mr. Benson presented 11 witnesses for the State and Mr. Breclaw presented 12 for Dr. Koo. Their testimony took 13 hours. Final arguments and sentencing took place Wednesday morning.

The State's first witness, an unmarried mother of three, was a patient of Dr. Koo for three years. She testified that every time she went to see him he fondled her breasts while checking her heart. Once, while she was laying on the exam table with her panties off, he injected her and she passed out. When she awoke her panties were still off. She admitted going to him just to get drugs (codeine) to satisfy her addiction.

The second witness for the State chose Dr. Koo from an HMO. Finding herself pregnant, she went to his Calumet City (Illinois) office in July 1988. She told of being raped on her third visit.

Her story brought back memories of the trial when she said, "He told me to put my feet in the stirrups. Then he pulled me down to the end of the table. There was a drape taped to the lamp that extended off the wall. He wiped me down with some gauze with alcohol or something on it, and then he inserted a speculum and took it out and then tried to insert something else that I didn't know what it was. Rosie (the office girl) was in the room standing next to me holding my arms. I thought it was for comfort, but I realize now that it was just to keep me from touching the drape. And then I realized that I was being sexually assaulted, and I sat back up on the table. He flushed me out with rubbing alcohol, left the room for a few minutes, and then returned.

"Rosie was still there. She seemed to be stalling for a while before she left the room. After Rosie left he said if I was interested in an abortion he would help me, and I told him I didn't need his help. I stood up to leave. He reached the door before I did and he told me that he loved me and didn't want anything to happen to me, and I grabbed the doorknob and left.

"On the way out Rosemary handed me a note which read, 'call me at home later tonight. We need to talk. My number is . . . I'm very suspicious. If that is going on, I'll quit now.'"

She then went to the hospital for a rape kit test, but did not confront the doctor because she was afraid, especially because Rosie had held her arms down. She said she just wanted to get out of there alive.

The results of her rape kit tests were negative, as to be expected after being flushed out. She could not tell if Koo had ejaculated inside her.

Cross-examination brought out the fact that at the time she was 22 years old and unmarried. Mr. Breclaw was unable to break her down or discredit her testimony. God knows, he tried. He tried in the most obnoxious and obscene manner possible.

Because she had testified to being sexually assaulted, the defense attorney felt he had the right to go into her sexual experience so as to judge her ability to recognize a sexual assault. He asked her how many times she had seen a penis, how many times she had a penis inside her, and how many times a man had ejaculated inside her.

Through it all she kept her cool. To his dismay, she answered each and every question with the self-assurance of a woman who was not the least bit embarrassed by either her testimony or the circumstances in which it was given. Still, he went on and on until Judge Page stopped him.

He then made the point that the Calumet City Police did not press charges because they had no evidence. Having been flushed out, she saw nothing unusual about that.

He next tried to convince the judge that a civil case she filed had also come up empty. He was stopped in his tracks when she testified to receiving an undisclosed sum of money from Dr. Koo's insurance carrier in settlement of the civil suit. The cross-examination ended on a lighter note.

* * *

Q.   "Now, Dr. Koo had a problem with the English language, did he not, expressing himself?"

A.   "I don't think so."

Q.   "You understood him very clearly?"

A.   "Yes, sir."

Q.   "And he didn't have an accent of any type that would prevent him from being understood?"

A.   "He has an accent but so do I."

Q.   "You do?"

A."   "I've been told."

Q.   "So in other words, in your opinion Dr. Koo speaks very clearly and succinctly and he is easily understood?"

A.   "From what I've heard him say, yes."

Q.   "Did you ever make the complaint to Rosie that you had been molested?"

A.   "Yes, I did."

Q.   "And when did you make that complaint to her?"

A.   "As I was walking out the door; I told her (in response to her note about quitting) yes, definitely, so she could pack her stuff."

* * *

The State's third witness was a patient of Dr. Koo from 1983 through 1986. She had never been married and the first of her two children was born in 1985. She testified to being raped by Dr. Koo in the fall of 1983, six months after she became his patient. She told her story in a clear, calm, matter-of-fact manner.

"It was at his Kennedy Avenue office in the second exam room. After I undressed he came into the room and told me to put my feet in the stirrups and scoot down to the edge of the table. I did, and for some reason he told me I wasn't relaxing. He said to take a couple of deep breaths, which I did, and he said, 'No, no, no, you still not relaxing. You're kind of tense. I'll give you a shot.' And he gave me a shot in the right arm.

"I never needed a shot before a pelvic exam before. It made me feel light-headed and as if I had a ton of bricks on my head. I could see okay, though, and still talk.

"Then he took the cloth and taped it to an overhead lamp that was at the foot of the bed. I thought he was proceeding with the pelvic examination, but I didn't feel anything cold, as far as the instrument or anything. The only thing unusual I noticed was I could see the top of his head and the top of his glasses. Him being short, I thought I shouldn't have because during the times I had pelvic exams, he usually pulled a stool up to the bottom of the table and I couldn't see him at all.

"It was strange. Normally there is some pressure from the instrument. I didn't feel any pressure that day. I felt something rubbing against the bottom, the underside of my thigh and the bottom of his jacket coat. I wasn't sure what was inside me because it wasn't a lot of pressure or fulfillment as if someone was having sex, but something was going on because it was some kind of rhythmic motion was going on back and forth inside me. "The table had some kind of a step, footstep at the bottom, and it seemed as if he stepped off because the table wasn't unbalanced, but it moved like some extra weight had been lifted off of it.

"Then he cleaned me out with some kind of warm solution or something. It wasn't real cold. Later I told my two aunts and a neighbor about it. I told them something strange happened. For some reason this exam was totally different, and I thought he had had sex with me.

"I didn't go to the police because I didn't think anyone would believe me. I was nineteen years old, you know, and who am I to say this doctor, this prominent man, supposedly had sex with me?"

Under cross-examination she stuck to her story. Mr. Breclaw did, however, manage to bring out the fact that she had continued to see Dr. Koo after that incident. It was an interesting lesson in human nature to hear her tell why.

* * *

Q. "And in fact after this occurred you then continued to go see Dr. Koo and continued to have further pelvic exams, did you not?"

A. "Yes."

Q. "Tell me why you would, after being raped in the fall of 1983 continue to go back to Dr. Koo's office and go through pelvic examinations where you had to take off your pants and your underpants and spread your legs and lay on an examining table and let the rapist continue to do pelvic examinations?"

A. "As far as his medical knowledge, he was a good doctor. Whenever I was sick, whatever he prescribed for me, it worked."

Q. "So you didn't mind the fact that he raped you?"

A. "I had a problem with it, but I wasn't quite sure as do I let this bother me or do I need to get well?"

Q. "So I ask you why would you go back to a doctor that had raped you, take off your pants and lie on an examining table and have him do a pelvic examination on you?"

A. "I'm not quite sure why."

Q. "I'll tell you why, because you were not raped."

A. "Oh, I know what happened to me that day. Any other time, any other pelvic exam was not different except for that day. I've had plenty of pelvic exams from Planned Parenthood, never had a problem. I didn't go to medical school. I didn't go to no medical school, but I know that someone had sex with me that I didn't consent to. Something was wrong that day. Something was very wrong that day."

Q. "Has your daughter been treated by Dr. Koo?"

A. "Up until she was two."

Q. "Can you tell me why you would take your daughter to be treated for a period of two years, until 1987, by the doctor that raped you in his examining room in the fall of 1983?"

A. "Well, I really hope he wouldn't rape a little baby if I was in the room with her. She was never alone in the room with him."

Q. "You trusted Dr. Koo between 1985 and 1987?"

A. "Usually trust most doctors when you go to them."

Q. "Even though, as you testified, he raped you in the fall of 1983?"

A. "Something happened and I believe it was rape."

Mr. Benson questioned her again to bring out the fact that she had never filed a civil suit, never filed criminal charges, and had absolutely nothing to gain by her testimony.

* * *

The fourth witness testified that on her first visit Dr. Koo had fondled her breast while "listening" to her heart. She returned for three more visits to get diet pills, but always with another woman. Nothing happened on those occasions. After four visits she stopped going to him. On cross-examination Mr. Breclaw brought out that she had been a friend of Tammy's for three years.

Mr. Benson's fifth witness went to Dr. Koo because of some lumps in her breast and some seepage. She did not like his manner and decided to look for another doctor. She later charged him with billing her insurance for work not performed.

Mr. Breclaw then objected to testimony about these charges. He said he failed to see the relevancy. Mr. Benson shot back with, "It's called insurance fraud, Your Honor, and it goes to his character." The sixth witness, a 28-year-old receptionist at Dr. Koo's Calumet City office, testified she was ordered to file insurance forms with surgical codes for procedures that never took place. She refused and the work was given to Dr. Koo's Hammond office. She added, "When I did quit, the other doctors told me not to get involved and I didn't want any problems. I didn't report any of this to anyone. I felt that no one would believe me."

The seventh witness for the State worked at the Illinois Department of Professional Regulation. Her job was to investigate allegations made against individuals and to monitor consent orders to see whether or not doctors placed on probation were abiding by the terms.

She testified about Dr. Koo's violation of a consent order that arose out of an incident with the second witness. Dr. Koo was ordered to have a third party present during pelvic exams, pay a $1,500 fine, and remain on probation for one year. The order took effect on September 1, 1989.

Dr. Koo neither renewed his Illinois licenses nor took the required classes. He closed his Illinois office and moved to Indiana.

Witness number eight was employed as an investigator and a law clerk for the attorney general's office, State of Indiana, in the division of consumer protection. She testified as follows.

"In response to information our office received from Illinois we notified the Indiana Medical Licensing Board of Dr. Koo's failure to abide by his probationary terms. Since Indiana gives full faith and credit to all actions of other licensing boards in the country, the Indiana board issued an Emergency Suspension, on January 24, 1991, of Dr. Koo's license to practice medicine in Indiana.

"An expedited hearing was held on February 5 and Dr. Koo's license was reinstated with some restrictions. One restriction was that he could not perform pelvic examinations on female patients. Another restriction required him to provide the patient with a notice, based on the Illinois form, that a third party must be present for any physical examination of female patients requiring the patient to disrobe. My office has also filed a petition with the Medical Licensing Board to suspend Dr. Koo's license based on his conviction for rape. Unlike Illinois, where a person convicted of a felony loses their right to practice medicine, a convicted felon in Indiana does not automatically lose his license to practice medicine."

The ninth witnesses, number seven in the parade of victims, testified to breast fondling and overbilling in May 1992. Her testimony took 28 pages of court transcripts to record.

Witness number 10 was Linda Cohen. On February 7, 1991 she had filed a formal complaint with the Hammond Police Department (Sgt. Hedinger) to the effect that Dr. Koo was having sex with her, by mutual consent, in his office. She later said the affair began in her home.

Early in July 1992, she signed a document at the Hammond Police Department dropping her complaint of February 1991, and stating that she never had sexual relations with Dr. Koo. At the time of the trial she told Mr. Benson that her first statement was correct and that she dropped the charges later under coercion from Dr. Koo.

Mr. Breclaw's position was that Linda's first statement was not true and that she had made the complaint to force Dr. Koo to give her financial help in a failing business venture that Dr. Koo had set up for Linda and her husband.

Mr. Breclaw "suggested" that the prosecutor's office had applied improper pressure in an unethical manner to get Linda to go back to her original story.

At the time of this testimony Linda was twenty-six, married and the mother of two children — a 7-year-old son and a 5-month-old daughter.

These basic facts were never in dispute. Other facts were very much in dispute. Yet it was not so much the facts of Linda's relationship with Dr. Koo as it was the motivation of each of the individuals that was being thrashed out in open court.

For rumor had it that Linda's daughter, reported to have oriental features, had been fathered by Dr. Koo. Whether or not that rumor was based on fact was open to speculation. But when Linda took her daughter to Dr. Koo for medical treatment, Dr. Koo did not treat her until after Linda had signed the second statement dropping her earlier complaint.

At first Mr. Benson wanted to have Linda testify to her relationship with the doctor so as to establish his character before the court and thus support the State's contention that he should be given the maximum sentence.

When Mr. Breclaw chose to attack the integrity of the prosecutor's office in general and Mr. Benson in particular, Mr. Benson wanted Linda to refute these allegations.

When he began Linda's direct examination by questioning her about her first statement to the Hammond police, counsel for the defense objected and the battle of the attorneys began.

* * *

MR. BRECLAW

"I would object, Your Honor. This witness apparently was unable to testify at trial on the matters contained in that statement as they relate to having sexual intercourse with Dr. Koo in his office. In fact, she broke down, and you indicated that she would not be a witness, that it would be cruel and unusual, cruel and harmful for her health to put her in a position of being a witness."

THE COURT

"I felt it would be cruel to have put her through that in front of a jury. I also felt that the jury would have been in a position of pure speculation because she was almost incoherent, but we're not at that state right now, and in terms of the statement itself, I've certainly seen it before, and I understand that you may want to cross-examine on it.

"If it should turn out that cross-examination is not available to you because of circumstances as they may develop during this hearing, then I of course cannot give the statement the same weight that I would fully cross-examined."

MR. BRECLAW

"I object to the whole procedure. Normally you ask questions of a witness and they answer these questions. But this witness has previously been unable to answer questions concerning — I'm asking rather than just introducing this statement, let's see if she will answer the questions."

THE COURT

"What is your objection to the statement?"

MR. BRECLAW

"First of all, that it's outside a normal procedure of how witnesses are questioned, and then in this case you're allowing hearsay, and then I have no problem with the statement itself going into evidence; however, prior to this hearing, during the hearing (July 28, 1992) to question whether or not her testimony would be admissible before the jury, she was unable to go forward and testify. So now the State is going through the back door with what they couldn't bring through the front door."

THE COURT

"Yes, but they're going through at the end of the proceedings rather than in the jury trial, and these are things which I believe the law suggests that my experience and discretion will help us sort through a little more carefully than we might do in front of a jury."

MR. BRECLAW

"It's very unfair."

THE COURT

"I'll keep it in mind during cross-examination, and I'll in fact not even look at the statement until such time as you've had an opportunity to cross-examine."

MR. BENSON

"Is the court then upholding the defendant's objection to the admission of that statement?"

THE COURT

"You had to ask. I guess I have to rule then. At the moment we have the statement before us. Since I'm not going to look at it now I'll take the motion for admission under advisement.

"And now, Mr. Benson, I might suggest that you may want to try some direct questions."

* * *

Mr. Benson did, and Linda answered, "I started seeing Dr. Koo in '85 after my first child. They did a C-section and didn't clean the afterbirth and so he cleaned it out. A little later I called Dr. Koo when I wasn't feeling well. I said I didn't have a car or anything, so he came to my house, and then we sat down. I had got him a cup of coffee, like he asked me, and then all of a sudden it led like one thing to another and we had sex."

Linda then testified that this relationship continued for a number of years, sometimes at her house, sometimes at his office. Never during that time did Dr. Koo have difficulty getting or maintaining an erection. Nor did he have any sexual problems during the years that the affair continued.

She noted that Dr. Koo gave her husband two examining tables from his office, tables that he said he no longer wanted. Then she finished up her direct testimony with the following.

"I didn't have menstruation, so then I went in to Dr. Koo and I told him that and he checked me. That was June of last year. He said I was pregnant.

"Sometime later he came to my house and asked me, well, do you think this baby belongs to me, and I had told Dr. Koo, I'm not going to say I can guarantee the baby is yours. I just don't want to talk about it, you know. I left it at that, and then I remember after that, when he asked me again when he came over another time. I told him I'm not standing here saying oh, yes, because, you know, a blood test will find out.

"Then he offered me $500 and told me he can take me to a clinic and get me an abortion, and I had told Dr. Koo that I was scared. I didn't want to get another abortion. After that I talked to a lawyer about a paternity action against him."

It was in cross-examination that it got nasty.

* * *

MR. BRECLAW

Q. "Ms. Cohen, you have indicated, have you not, to the police and to the State of Indiana that you did not wish to testify in this matter?

A. "Yes, I did."

Q. "By your appearance here today have you been coerced by the prosecutor in coming here to testify?"

A. "No, I just know that — if I can explain something —"

Q. "That's all right. Just let me ask the questions. Has anyone told you that if you didn't come here and testify that you would be put in jail?"

A. "No."

Q. "No one has ever told you that?"

A. "No."

Q. "Are you sure?"

A. "Can you explain that to me, John?"

Q. "Call me Mr. Breclaw, please."

A. "I mean, Breclaw."

THE COURT

"Well, I see. I take it you two —"

MR. BRECLAW

"You take it wrong."

THE COURT

"I just — I didn't mean it that way, Jack. I just wanted to make sure that apparently this is a witness who has spoken frequently with both sides in the case. Am I misunderstanding?"

MR. BRECLAW

"That's accurate."

THE COURT

"I assumed that that was the extent of her knowing you by your first name."

MR. BRECLAW

Q. " Mrs. Cohen, had you on several occasions called my office to tell me that you did not want to testify but that the prosecutor's office was threatening and coercing you into appearing to testify against Dr. Koo?"

A.   "I was getting, you know, harassed because it was so on me I was ready for a nervous breakdown."

Q.   "Who was harassing you?"

A.   "I was harassed by the State."

* * *

At this point Mr. Benson objected and Judge Page suggested another line of questioning might develop the point he was trying to make in a more concise manner.

* * *

MR. BRECLAW

"I am conducting cross-examination."

THE COURT

"I don't mean to hinder you at all from that, Mr. Breclaw. It's just that if we could get to the essence of the matter."

MR. BRECLAW

"If this was a normal witness with both oars in the water I would proceed in that manner, but this is a woman that has problems."

THE COURT

"Well, it's actually for that reason that I was suggesting that you proceed the other way, but as you suggest, you have the right to conduct your cross-examination in your own way."

MR. BRECLAW

Q. "Did you believe Mr. Benson was threatening you?"

A. "I just felt I was being harassed, and when I said I didn't want to come in the first place, then I got a subpoena, and, you know, I mean, I didn't understand because I had dropped the complaint and everything against Dr. Koo. I don't understand, you know; I'm confused."

Q. "And did you feel threatened by the prosecutor?"

A. "Yes, I did."

Q. "In your signed statement of July of 1992 you stated, "I have no sexual relations with Dr. Koo whatsoever, and I'm not against him in any way. Instead, he has done everything to help me." Is that true?"

A. "The part that is not true, where I tried to explain to Donna, (Dr. Koo's receptionist), but she typed up on there that I had no sex with Dr. Koo whatsoever."

Q. "I, Linda Cohen, do hereby confess that the statements made at my deposition were not true. I was very confused as to what I was saying." Is that true?"

A. "Yes, but the part, if I can —"

Q. "Let me read on. "Prior to the depositions I had went to the police department to drop all complaints against Dr. Koo; therefore, I was very scared and very nervous and was going through family and business problems at the time, along with some financial difficulty." Is that true?"

A. "Yes, but the part about stating I had no sexual relationship with Dr. Koo whatsoever, that part was not true."

Q. "You did have sexual relationships with Dr. Koo, and they were consensual relationships?"

A. "Yes."

Q.   "And then you state, "The above statements are true and correct, and they have been made of my own free will."

A.   "Yes, because like I said, at that time when I signed this, my baby daughter was real sick. I took her in to Dr. Koo, and before I could take her in there, Donna said she had to talk to you (Breclaw) and ask if it was okay, and then she said she had to talk to Dr. Koo to see if it was okay, so I went ahead and took the baby on in, and I signed the paper before I could get medical treatment for my baby."

Q.   "Did Dr. Koo treat your baby that day?"

A.   "Yes, he did."

Q.   "While you were living with your husband you were having sex with Dr. Koo at your home?"

A.   "Yes."

Q.   "And your husband was aware that you were having sex with Dr. Koo at your home?"

A.   "When he caught him, yes."

Q.   "This was prior to your giving the statement to the police?"

A.   "Yes."

Q.   "In October of 1990 did Dr. Koo introduce you to or deliver a business proposition to you and your husband about operating a restaurant in Chicago?"

A.   "The restaurant, yes, in Chicago."

Q.   "And did you in fact sign a lease and then go to Chicago with your husband and live above the restaurant and run the business?"

A.   "Yes, for about six months."

*   *   *

Mr. Breclaw then developed the point that Linda and her husband were $6000 behind in rent payments to the landlord of the restaurant. He attempted to show that Linda had tried to get Dr. Koo to pay the back rent and, when he didn't, Linda then filed her complaint with the Hammond police out of spite. He also suggested that Linda was afraid she would lose her house in Hammond, or, at best, have a lien placed on it by the Chicago landlord. Linda insisted that Dr. Koo had told her and her husband that they did not have to pay rent. She said that the day before she had gone to the police with her first complaint Dr. Koo had come to her apartment in Chicago to tell her he was in big trouble because a woman was accusing him of rape. Mr. Breclaw suggested that Linda's motivation for her complaint was to force Dr. Koo to pay the back rent.

He further suggested that Linda had never had sex with Dr. Koo but had made that accusation simply out of spite when Dr. Koo had not given her the money. Linda denied it all.

She was beginning to break up under the questioning. The Judge recessed the court for several minutes to let her pull herself together. She was sobbing out of control. Shortly after the court resumed, Mr. Breclaw finished and Mr. Benson took Linda on redirect.

*   *   *

MR. BENSON

Q. "You said that you went down to the police station to drop some charges, correct?"

A. "Yes, and the police told me once I drop the complaint I don't have to go to court."

Q. "Now, are you saying that what you told the police was a lie or that you just didn't want to press charges?"

A. "I just didn't want to press charges. I didn't want to, you know, go through court and everything else."

Q. "The statement that you gave Detective Hedinger, isn't that in fact a true statement?"

A. "Right, everything is true except the part where the sexual intercourse began."

Q. "Now, you said that someone from the prosecutor's office coerced you or harassed you or threatened you. Is that what you're telling this court?"

A.   "It's not like threats. I mean, it's like I was just — I felt
      like I was being harassed. I was a nervous wreck. I al-
      most had a breakdown."

Q.   "Isn't it true that you talked to our office and you asked
      me to tell the defense attorney to stop harassing you?"

A.   [Witness sobs.]

* * *

Linda is in a state of total breakdown. The judge tries to calm
her down but is unable to do so. Several minutes go by before he
allows Mr. Benson to continue. When he restates his last question,
Linda falls apart — sobbing out of control.

* * *

THE COURT

"I would suggest that we are through both direct and cross-examination, and you may want to consider just how important the
testimony is at this point."

MR. BENSON

"Judge, I place nothing above the integrity of the prosecutor's
office, and I ask for permission to continue on with this line of
questioning. They have directly tried to impute the integrity of this
office, and I believe I should have the right to clear that up."

THE COURT

"I would simply say that I have understood the evidence as indicating that Ms. Cohen was required by your office to come testify, even maybe when she didn't want to. I have not understood it
as more than that. I have not understood her as saying that it was
more than that."

"Mr. Breclaw, correct me if I'm wrong, but I believe that that
is what she said — it wasn't really threatening."

MR. BRECLAW

"I don't quite agree with that characterization."

THE COURT

"How would you characterize it?"

MR. BRECLAW

"I would characterize it that it was implied to her that she had to testify along the lines as was stated in her statement to the police on February 7, 1991. That's what she was being called to testify to, and that's what they expected her to testify to."

THE COURT

"Does either side have any evidence which would tend to suggest to me that this witness has been threatened into lying to this court? So far as I have been able to hear she's only been threatened, as you have characterized it, into telling the truth."

MR. BRECLAW

"You've heard her cross-examination and her motives, her financial motives, and her business motives for testifying. That's something that the trier of fact would have to determine whether or not she's telling the truth. Whether or not in fact she did have sex with Dr. Koo, even on a consensual basis."

THE COURT

"Are you asking me that?"

MR. BRECLAW

"Judge, I've just placed the evidence in front of this court. You're the one that has to make that decision. I am done with my examination."

THE COURT

"That's what I thought. What I'm asking is how far you wish to press it with this witness, Mr. Benson. She's not handling it well at this point, and you have to decide how important it is."

MR. BENSON

"Well, Judge, with all due respect to the court, I'm not going to let defense counsel sit here and ask the witness how often did Mr. Benson harass you. I'm going to clear that up. She's just going to have to compose herself because I want that question answered. He does not have the right to say that on cross-examination and I don't get a chance to redirect."

THE COURT

"Mr. Benson, I don't want you to take this personally, but I've already understood her to answer it by saying she didn't feel she was threatened. Those were her exact words."

MR. BENSON

"Then I want to know what she meant by harassing her."

THE COURT

"Let's give her a moment, and perhaps that question would be appropriate as to what she meant by the word, but there does come a point where we have to take into account how important our own personal honor as attorneys is when the witness is in this state."

MR. BENSON

"This goes above any individual honor as an attorney. This is the reputation of this office."

THE COURT

"I don't see it that way, but I can understand where you might. I haven't understood it to have that significance. Mrs. Cohen, take a moment. Wipe your eyes and take a few deep breaths, if you would, please. We're almost through. I have a question for you. Earlier you said that you felt that the prosecutor's office or people in it might have been harassing you. What exactly did you mean when you said that?"

THE WITNESS

A." Just, you know, getting the subpoena and everything, and then I felt I didn't want to come, and I'm getting a subpoena after I dropped the complaint."

THE COURT

"Okay, Mr. Benson."

MR. BENSON

"Can I ask a question of the witness?"

THE COURT

"You can try."

MR. BENSON

Q. "Ms. Cohen, did our office ever threaten you or tell you what to say when you came into this courtroom?"

A. "No."

Q. "And in fact didn't I tell you to tell the truth?"

A. "Yes."

Q. "And I never told you what to say, other than the truth?"

A. "The truth, right."

MR. BENSON

"I have nothing further."

10
Judgment by Page

Since the laws of the State of Indiana permit a victim of a felony to take an active role in the sentencing of the convicted felon, Tammy Spasske Garza could accept or decline each of two options.

She could testify under oath, subject to cross-examination, as to how her life had been altered by the rape. And, after all witnesses had testified, she could make an unsworn statement, with no cross-examination, on the same subject. She chose to exercise both options.

As the eleventh witness for the State, she began by saying, "I've been going through hell. I've had nightmares constantly since the first day. I have trouble getting to sleep. My husband can't even come to bed if I am asleep because I'll wake up fighting like, scared.

"I don't trust doctors at all. Before the trial I was afraid he would do something, so my husband changed the locks and added dead bolts and motion detector lights to make me feel safer.

"I've been humiliated by people that still think he's innocent. I've become a victim again. People at work ignore me. Some people give me dirty looks. One former patient, a nice old lady, was going to testify that he was a good doctor. I told her he raped me. She was never called, but then, after the guilty verdict, I asked her if she really was going to testify. And she just yelled, yes, yes, and she started yelling at me, go away, go away, and back up like I was going to hurt her. I yelled right back. I said, 'Your doctor is a convicted rapist.'

"I want him to admit it; he raped me. I am the victim. I want his sentence to be the maximum — 20 years. He took away my life. I want his tooken away. I want him to rot in jail."

* * *

MR. BRECLAW

> Q. "You've testified that because of this rape that you can't sleep at night, is that correct?"
>
> A. "Yes."
>
> Q. "Isn't it a fact that part of you're not sleeping at night is attributable to the other two men that you have accused of rape in your life?"

MR. BENSON

"Defense counsel is intentionally trying to smear this witness's reputation by bringing that up, and he knows that it has no bearing on this hearing and it would not be admissible in a trial. And he knows it is not a proper statement to make."

THE COURT

"This witness has previously been the victim of a rape, and that is a matter of the records that have been submitted in the court. I in fact intended to take that into account, and it is not something that I can put out of my mind. I will allow the question to be put — are these nightmares the result of other things in your life or this alone?"

THE WITNESS

"No."

THE COURT

"Is it this alone?"

THE WITNESS

"Yes."

MR. BRECLAW

"Now, you have accused two other men in your life of rape, have you not, Mrs. Spasske?"

MR. BENSON

"Objection, Your Honor, same grounds. The court has inquired as to the cause of her nightmares. He's going to harp on this as long as the court lets him, trying to make her look like garbage."

THE COURT

"The truth is you're going to continue to harp on it?"

MR. BRECLAW

"No, the truth is that she made two other accusations of rape against two other men; that she is not protected by the Rape Shield Act now — only before a jury. The purpose is to ask whether or not in each of those other rape accusations she suffered from a loss of sleep."

THE COURT

"Just ask her that way."

MR. BRECLAW

Q.   "With respect to the rape accusation that you made in 1979, Mrs. Garza, did you suffer a lack of sleep because of those rape accusations?"

A.   "Probably. I was 18; I don't remember."

Q.   "How long did the loss of sleep because of that 1979 rape accusation go on?"

A.   "I don't know."

MR. BENSON

"I'm going to object to this entire line of questioning."

THE COURT

"You're going to have to take it question by question. I understand where you're coming from, Mr. Benson, and you are correct in saying I will not allow this to be used as an opportunity to pillory this victim. She stands before the court as the victim of a rape. It's an established fact.

"Now, there will be limits on the amount of questions that will be asked, but certain questions are allowable. I have sustained your last objection. Mr. Breclaw."

MR. BRECLAW

Q.   "With respect to the 1979 alleged rape, that individual was never prosecuted, was he?"

MR. BENSON

"Objection, that's the exact same question, Your Honor, irrelevant."

THE COURT

"Sustained."

MR. BRECLAW

Q.   "As a result of that rape, did you suffer any mental torment?"

A.   "You never get over rape totally."

Q.   "So what you're telling me is that part of what you're feeling today against Dr. Koo is a result of the rape that you had in 1979?"

A.   "No."

Q.   "Now, let's go to the allegation or accusation of rape against your ex-boyfriend."

A.   "I never accused him of rape."

Q.   "The mental torment that you are suffering now that you testified to because of Dr. Koo's action in raping you, is this the same — is this mental torment attributable to a statement of rape that you made to the people at —"

MR. BENSON

"Objection, Your Honor. It's outside the scope of the sentencing hearing, assuming facts not in evidence, Your Honor."

MR. BRECLAW

"If I may finish the question?"

MR. BENSON

"The question contains the answer, and he'll have it in and won his battle. If he wants to embarrass her in front of these people, he's doing it, okay, and that's exactly —"

BY MR. BRECLAW

"My client is facing 20 years in prison. There is the family."

MR. BENSON

"That is exactly what she said —"

THE WITNESS

"He deserves it."

MR. BENSON

"— when she said she continues to be the victim."

MR. BRECLAW

"You rape easy, Mrs. Spasske, I would think."

THE COURT

"Mr. Breclaw."

THE WITNESS

"You shut up [to Breclaw]."

THE COURT

"You be quiet yourself."

THE COURT

"Mr. Breclaw, I expect you as you stand there now as a gentleman to apologize for what you just said."

MR. BRECLAW

"I apologize to the court as an officer of the court."

THE COURT

"You apologize to the witness as well, Mr. Breclaw [long pause]. Mr. Breclaw."

MR. BRECLAW

"Now we're in confrontation, right?"

THE COURT

"I'm afraid so. You've gone too far, and I have an obligation to protect a victim, and I must insist."

MR. BRECLAW

"I've got to think about it for a moment, to be honest with you."

* * *

There followed much more than a moment. Several minutes went by without a sound from John Breclaw. Finally his assistant counsel, Jay Binder, leaned over to speak to him. It was evident that Mr. Breclaw was unable to talk his way out of this situation in any manner that would salvage any face at all. He was not going to offer a personal apology to Tammy and he faced certain discipline from the court if he did not. Mr. Binder provided the way out.

* * *

MR. BRECLAW

"Your Honor, contrary to my feelings, I realize that was an improper question. Mrs. Garza, as I am an officer of the court, regardless of what my personal feelings are, that particular question was improper to you, and I apologize for it as an officer of the court."

THE COURT

"Thank you, Mr. Breclaw. You're a gentleman for having done so."

MR. BRECLAW

Q. "Let's get back to 1988 when you presented yourself to the Hammond Clinic for an AIDS test and alleged to the doctor who examined you that you were raped by your boyfriend."

MR. BENSON

"Objection, Your Honor. How many times do I have to object to the same question?"

THE COURT

"It's hard to say. I suppose as many times as it's asked. Mr. Breclaw, what is the purpose of this questioning?"

MR. BRECLAW

"I want to find out if the same torment she has today is attributable to a statement that she made to a doctor and nurse at the Hammond Clinic when she presented herself for an AIDS test in 1988."

THE COURT

"Did you understand? Is it part of what you're suffering?"

THE WITNESS

"No."

THE COURT

"Mr. Breclaw."

MR. BRECLAW

Q.   "This is a different torment, is that right, Mrs. Garza?"

A.   "Yes."

* * *

During the remaining three hours of the evening session Mr. Breclaw presented a series of character witnesses. Most of them testified to Dr. Koo's good character.

Judge Page took a moment to express his general displeasure with the licensing authorities of Illinois and Indiana. He felt the medical profession was not doing a good job of investigating problems within their ranks and he said so in open court. He was extremely upset that the legal profession was left to clean up the medical mess.

A lady who appeared to be Dr. Koo's wife sat in the front row. Her facial expression was frozen as she kept putting her arm about her daughter, Jenny Koo, who was sobbing for most of the session. The doctor's son, Cannon Koo, sat on the other side of his mother. Both the Koo children testified as to their love of their father and that he was a good family man. Jenny said she was a strong advocate of women's rights and could not believe her father had done anything wrong. It was a sad sight.

The Judge announced that he had received some 800 letters, mostly from Chicago's Korean community, testifying to Dr. Koo's character. Many believed he had been convicted because of his race.

The schedule for Wednesday's session, beginning at 10:00 a.m. called for Tammy to make her unsworn statement, Dr. Koo to make his, Mr. Benson to present final arguments in support of a maximum sentence, and Mr. Breclaw likewise for a minimum one.

* * *

THE COURT

"Yesterday the victim in this case, Ms. Garza, testified and made a statement as to what she felt was appropriate. At this time, Ms. Garza, do you have anything to add?"

MS. GARZA

"Yes, sir. That I have been the victim in this case. My whole life has been turned upside down, and it's become hell because of this and especially yesterday, and I am not only a victim of Koo, but I also have been a victim of Breclaw. What he said to me was totally uncalled for [turning to Mr. Breclaw]. You had the audacity to say that."

MR. BRECLAW

"If the shoe fits, wear it, Mrs. Spasske."

MR. BENSON

"Judge, I would ask the court to instruct defense counsel."

THE COURT

"John, please don't make it any more difficult than it is."

MR. BRECLAW

"I don't think I can."

THE COURT

"I understand, and I ask you for patience. The statutes require that I give her the chance, and basically as long as it's just words, she can say it, and that means that people like you and I must sit back and take it.

"Anything further?"

MS. GARZA

"Just about everybody here today is saying that they believe he's innocent. This isn't for saying he's innocent or not. He is a convicted rapist."

THE COURT

"Young Soo Koo, you stand before the court convicted of rape, a Class B felony. What, if anything, do you wish to say before judgment is pronounced?"

THE DEFENDANT

"Thank you very much, Your Honor, ladies and gentlemen, for giving me this chance to say something about my feeling.

"I read my letter to you, sir.

"Dear Judge, I'm accused of the horrible things, and also I was — I am convicted of that horrible things. I'm a physician. I have dedicated my life to helping others. I have treated many patients for many years without payment, but I continue to visit my patients in their home. I'll do the same. Caring my patients and the respect of patients was my primary pay. It was my life.

"I care for Tammy's family for past 10 years. Most of my patient were not wealthy, and also my services given without charge. I thought that I had this respect and affections. I thought I had earned this. My lawyer told me I could not testify because my poor broke English may cause misunderstanding. Still I heard this things being said to me. I want to cry out, but I didn't, but I cry out with my hurt inside.

"I do not know why Tammy would say such things against me. I am broken that she would say that, and I am broken that they will believe. I am a very good man. You can see man like me in the world. I'm very sorry to be here.

"I'm also sorry for expense and heartbreak that has been caused. I did not make intention wrong, but I was wrong, if I can say it, just not to have nurse all the time present. I cannot change my mistake, nor can I change my mind. I hope, I pray that you will see me at least in some part as a good man who had tried to contribute and to do his share in helping peoples, and that you consider me as this whole man, as you must sentence me.

"I just pray for the fact I'm totally innocent, and I have no doubt that I'm not guilty for this allegation with all my heart. Thank you. God bless you."

THE COURT

"Dr. Koo, you have said something that requires me to ask a question or two, if I might, of you that I did not ask during the trial. You have indicated that you did not testify."

THE DEFENDANT

"That's correct, sir.

THE COURT

"That was something that you talked about with your attorneys beforehand? You talked with Mr. Breclaw and Mr. Binder about that?

THE DEFENDANT

"Yes, sir.

* * *

August 26 • Wednesday • late morning

Mr. Benson took 45 minutes for a final argument to support the State's request for the maximum sentence allowed by law. He cited several sentencing precedents — the forethought and manner employed by the perpetrator; his systematic thought process and efforts to cover up his crime; his exploitation of the victim's trust; his violation of trust; the psychological trauma inflicted on his victim; his prior uncharged conduct; and the effect his crime had on the community.

In reference to the many character witnesses who testified for Dr. Koo, he said, "The Court cannot consider his character — he has none."

Turning to face Dr. Koo, the prosecutor announced, "Dr. Koo, you rape often!"

He then asked the Court to impose the maximum sentence of 20 years in prison.

Mr. Breclaw's final argument lasted 50 minutes. He asked for forgiveness, compassion, and prayer. He expressed Dr. Koo's thanks to the Korean community for their support and said the verdict was not racial — two Korean War veterans on the jury as evidence.

He was disappointed that the Rape Shield Act in Indiana kept him from using evidence of prior rapes involving the plaintiff. He mentioned his intention to appeal. Without an admission of guilt and lacking physical evidence, he felt there was some doubt.

He asked the court to consider the good things in the doctor's life. So as not to waste the doctor's medical talents, he suggested Dr. Koo, if sent to prison, should be sent to a minimum security prison and used to process incoming prisoners — giving physical exams and the like.

He said, "If my client is guilty he is a sick man who did a sick thing, not a bad man who did a bad thing."

He recommended the minimum sentence of six years, noting that Mike Tysen had just received eight years for raping a young woman in his hotel room. In an uncharacteristic display of common decency, Mr. Breclaw did not ask that the sentence be suspended.

The State of Indiana had mounted a massive effort to bring Dr. Koo to justice. Its cost was high; the allocation of time and resources enormous. The Honorable T. Edward Page now revealed the result of that expenditure.

He addressed the court by saying, "Doctors hold a special place. They are held to a higher standard of conduct. There has been a pattern of abuse by this doctor that indicates he has violated his trust. The doctor did some selecting of his victims. He gave some thought before he grabbed a breast.

"The sentence I impose will never be accepted by those who believe in Dr. Koo's innocence. His colleagues tell us he is a man to be respected, but they tell us they did not know of his dark side, and it is that dark side I address."

* * *

YOUNG SOO KOO WAS SENTENCED TO TWENTY YEARS IN PRISON.

Conclusion

Det. Sgt. Hedinger was now able to talk to the press about his nine-year investigation of Dr. Koo, who he referred to as a "serial rapist" who had arranged for his victims to come to him for at least 10 years. According to the Hammond detective, Koo came to the United States in 1973, built a medical practice that netted $200,000 a year, drove a Mercedes, lived in a $500,000 house, and owned $2.5 million in real estate. His investigations also covered alleged Medicaid fraud and illicit prescriptions of drugs. In addition to the prior victims who agreed to testify, Hedinger noted that 10 other victims had called to tell their stories but were afraid to testify. "It's not often you get two shots at a serial rapist," he told the *Post-Tribune* on August 27, 1992.

(Court records indicate that Young Soo Koo testified on his own behalf, without a translator, before that grand jury. His attorney at that time was John Breclaw.)

During the next eight months I gathered what information was available (notes from another juror, newspaper articles, interviews) and constructed a basic outline of this book. In November 1993, I obtained copies of 1,800 pages of trial transcripts selected from the total of 8,000.

In March, 1994, I was present at the Indiana Court of Appeals hearing of oral arguments, held at Indiana University's School of law in Indianapolis and open to the general public.

Dr. Koo's attorney advanced eight errors in the conduct of the trial that were judged serious enough to be grounds for appeal. The court saw fit to deal with four of them in oral arguments. The most significant were the "gender strike" and the admissibility of testimony from Martha Mason and Susan Long.

I then learned that early in the trial (Wednesday evening, July 15, 1992) Mr. Breclaw had moved for a mistrial on the basis that the court denied him the right to exercise peremptory challenges on two female jurors. Judge Page based this denial on a Supreme Court ruling that applied to the use of peremptory challenges to exclude potential jurors on the basis of race.

One of the appellate judges wondered aloud if further extension might not be the death knell of such challenges. The other two judges noted a singular lack of guidance from either Indiana's constitution or its statues.

The testimony of prior victims was covered next. The general consensus of the court seemed to be that normally such testimony would not be admissible. In this case, however, Mr. Breclaw had offered the positive defense of a drug-induced sexual fantasy. That seemed to open the door for rebuttal from the State. The court noted that such testimony in this case raised the question of whether or not three people would have identical fantasies.

The hearing ended with no clue as to the ultimate decision.

One judge indicated their deliberations would be completed before year end.

A bit of the mental burden was lifted from the Court of Appeals when, on April 19, 1994, the U.S. Supreme Court (in a 6-3 opinion written by Justice Harry Blackmun) ruled that people cannot be excluded from juries solely because of their sex. Judge Page, in his denial of Breclaw's challenge of two women on the Koo jury, had correctly predicted this extrapolation of a similar ruling concerning race. (Lora was one of the jurors involved.)

A week after oral arguments I received a call from Tammy Garza in a belated response to my January 1993 request for an interview concerning this book. Tammy now wanted input. She reviewed the manuscript with her husband, Jimmy, and made a number of suggestions and corrections which I accepted.

My respect for Tammy continued to grow in our subsequent conversations. In a taped interview with me she mentioned a significant change in the attitude of the Hammond police from the time of her first rape (1979) to that of Koo's (1989).

The first incident took place as she was returning home from a party she attended with her sister. The sister wanted to stay late; Tammy wanted to go. Thus, shortly after midnight, Tammy was walking along Kennedy Avenue (a main street in Hammond) when a man approached her, dragged her into an alley, and raped her. She was 18.

She wandered around in a daze for two hours before working up the courage to go home. Her father called the police and they sent an officer to the house. He told Tammy that she had "asked for it" by being out alone that late at night — dressed in jeans and a sweater! Her father threw the cop out of the house and the matter was dropped.

In 1989, 10 years later, when another police officer came to her house to take her statement, Tammy was hesitant to make a formal charge. This police officer asked, "What if this had happened to your daughter?" The rest, as they say, is history.

She also managed to clear up a little mystery for me that began during her testimony Wednesday afternoon when she requested a break in the trial. She related the following.

"Breclaw just kept hammering and hammering. He like kept badgering me over and over. And he got to me and I just lost it. I was basically hysterical. I asked for a break. It was the only time I asked for a break, and they didn't even wait for the jury to leave — they just let me go.

"I went down to the prosecutor's office. And we were all there — Phil Benson, Detective Hedinger and Jerry Cunningham. I told them I wanted to leave, I wanted to go home. And they told me whatever I wanted. If I wanted to leave, it was up to me. They had no problem with that. You want to do that, go home. Get Jimmy and go. Get in the car and go. And then Phil looked at me and said, 'By the way, Tammy, what size shoe do you wear?' "I had no idea what he was talking about and I just said, 'Nine, why?'

"And he said, 'That size nine fits nicely up Breclaw's ass.'

"I smiled. That's all it took. I felt determined and I said, 'Okay, let's go kick some butt.' And we went back upstairs to the court-room.

"And when I was sitting there waiting for the jury to come back, I started to get apprehensive and uneasy, and Phil Benson just pointed at his shoe and I started laughing."

Tammy then went on about how well she was treated by Phil. The first prosecutor didn't really believe her story and was too busy running for judge to spend much time on her case. When he got elected, he turned the 23-month-old case over to Benson.

According to Tammy, "He believed in me one hundred per-cent. Even stuff . . . I wasn't aware of it, but if you tell him any-thing, and it's a lie, he has the obligation to tell the other side. There were situations when I told him things, and it turned out I was telling him the truth, and I said to him, 'And you took that risk that I might have been lying?' "

"And he said, 'Yes, I believe in you one hundred percent.'

"And I could have been lying, and if I was lying, the informa-tion, by law, had to be turned over to Breclaw's side. Phil believed in me from the start. And Detective Hedinger, too. They believed in me one hundred percent.

"You asked about what I would say to other women. The only thing I can think of is that I hope women come forward. That they know it may be tough. This was the hardest thing I've ever had to do in my entire life, but it was worth it, and you can win."

Would she do it again, if she had to? "Oh, yes," she said, "In a heartbeat."

Concerning the civil suit, she said, "Nothing happened with that. It was known from day one that if I had to make a choice between the civil suit and the criminal, I wanted his butt behind bars. I never received any money and I never will. I won't go through another trial for the money. It's just not worth it."

On September 22, 1994, the Fifth District Court of Appeals of Indiana handed down an opinion that upheld the conviction of Young Soo Koo. The Honorable T. Edward Page, Judge Pro Tempore of the Superior Court of Lake County, was vindicated.

On October 27, 1994, in a conference room at the Indiana Government Center in Indianapolis the Medical Licensing Board of Indiana revoked the medical license of Young Soo Koo. An attorney representing Koo witnessed the proceeding but did not oppose the action.

Under Indiana law Koo can apply for reinstatement in seven years. It is not uncommon for Indiana to reinstate a revoked or suspended license to practice medicine — albeit with a variety of restrictions often difficult to enforce. That same day they reinstated doctors who had been personally involved with child molestation, drug addiction, and abuse of alcohol.

* * *